DYING TO LIVE

By Dr. Steven A. Jirgal

DEDICATION

This book is dedicated to families—real families.

- ~ The kind of families that stay together both in the good and bad times.

- ~ The kind of families that have learned the virtues of love, forgiveness, and generosity.

- ~ Families that will laugh and cry together without hesitation.

- ~ Families that will celebrate victories and overcome obstacles together.

- ~ Families that are united so strongly that time, tide, and trials can't pull them apart.

May God bless our country with these types of families!

INTRODUCTION

In the summer of 1987 I met Charlie. He was a high school football coach from a nearby county and was working as a clinician at a week-long quarterback camp. I served as the camp trainer. We looked beyond our differences in race and hit it off immediately.

Charlie was a good bit older than I am, wore a perpetual smile, and always seemed to have something good to say. He bounced around from group to group instructing and encouraging the young men in his charge. I always looked forward to camp season when Charlie would roll onto campus and we would pick right up where we left off.

One day I asked Charlie if he knew about the lions and gazelles in Africa. His puzzled look gave me the go ahead to share an old African proverb.

"Every morning in Africa, a gazelle wakes up.
It knows that it must outrun the fastest lion, or it will be killed.
Every morning in Africa, a lion wakes up.
It knows that it must outrun the slowest gazelle, or it will starve.
It does not matter whether you are a lion or a gazelle.
When the sun comes up, you had better be running."

That became a strong bridge in our relationship. Whenever we ran into each other or talked on the phone, part of our conversation included, "Every morning in Africa,…"

Then one day, I received a call from one of my friends in coaching. He told me that Charlie had cancer and was undergoing treatment. Things did not look good.

Charlie was admitted to the V.A. hospital, and I began making trips there to see him. Not a visit went by where we didn't talk about the lions and gazelles in Africa.

Charlie's condition deteriorated quickly. It seems like just yesterday I made my last trip to see him.

I quietly entered the dimly lit room finding my friend resting comfortably. I softly called his name and he opened his eyes a little and smiled.

Because he was so weak, I didn't stay long but did all of the talking. I prayed with him and gave him a hug. He squeezed my hand and whispered, "Every morning."

So once again and for the last time, I told him,

"Every morning in Africa, a gazelle wakes up.
It knows that it must outrun the fastest lion, or it will be killed.
Every morning in Africa, a lion wakes up.
It knows that it must outrun the slowest gazelle, or it will starve.
It does not matter whether you are a lion or a gazelle.
When the sun comes up, you had better be running."

Then I leaned over and kissed his forehead and said goodbye. He turned his head my way, smiled, and nodded.

A couple of days later, I got a call from his wife. She let me know that Charlie had passed on during the night.

Being a Pastor, spending time with someone as he dies is not unusual. I've watched some pass away gracefully, while others leave with great struggle. But over the years as I've watched so many people live and die, I've come to four main conclusions:

1. Statistics show that one out of every one person dies. No one gets out of here alive.

2. There never is a convenient time to die.

3. Unfinished business is the hallmark of every life.

4. People generally die the way they live, and those who best know how to live are most prepared to die.

Perhaps by the reading of this book, you will grasp the need to prepare for that which visits us all. My prayer is that in your preparation you will embrace those close to you and leave a positive mark on them that time cannot erase.

"DYING TO LIVE"

THURSDAY, MARCH 6

Tom sat in Dr. Matthew Riley's office for what seemed like a year. *At least he's got the temperature up in here,* Tom thought, reflecting on how cold the examination room always was. He wondered what was so urgent that he had been called to come by without delay. Tom had known Matt for many years. He and his physician had been friends since their college days. They had lost touch for several years while Matt was at medical school and Tom was working on his Masters in Business and establishing a career in Pharmaceutical sales. When Tom learned that Matt would be starting a practice just two towns away, he was elated. It didn't take long for the pair to pick up where they had left off and continue their strong friendship.

This was Tom's second visit to Matt's office in two weeks. The first was in response to Tom feeling fatigued. The nurse didn't sound anxious when she phoned and asked him to come in. Still, Tom wished that Marcie were there. He knew she was out running errands all day and silently scolded himself for not getting her cell phone fixed that morning.

Matt entered the room and Tom stood up extending his hand. As their eyes met Tom noticed that Matt's ready smile was conspicuously absent. "It's always good to see you Matt," Tom said sitting back down, "Now what's so important that you had me race down here?"

Matt walked around his desk, sat down in his burgundy leather chair, and opened the file he had brought with him. "Tom," Matt began, looking deeply at his friend, "I can sincerely say that there are only a few days in my life when

I wish I weren't me. This is one of them. I can't tell you how many times I had the lab check and re-check your test results, but it keeps coming back the same way." Shaking his head, Matt continued, "Tom, you've got a very rare disease known as 'leukopapliomegitis.' It is an extremely aggressive form of blood disorder, and while we can treat it to some degree, it is essentially terminal."

Tom looked up in disbelief. "Terminal? What do you mean, terminal?"

Matt pursed his lips not wanting to continue. "What I mean is there is absolutely no cure. We have no way of stopping the disease. It may, however, be possible to slow it down. Most people expire before they come in for medical treatment. That's why we have so little research available. You don't have much time."

"Tom," Matt continued, "I wish there was a mistake. But there is no mistake. As best as I can calculate, without medication you've got about six weeks. We've got some drugs that are experimental. The indications are that they may prolong your life for a few months. I can't tell you how much I wish it were different."

The words hit Tom like a sledgehammer and kept pounding in his ears like the haunting sound of a distant drum. *Six weeks, no mistake. Six weeks-no mistake. Six weeks, six weeks, six weeks. How is that possible?* Tom thought with his eyes glazing over as he stared at the floor. *What about Marcie and the kids? How can this be happening?* It seemed like forever before Tom could speak. "I don't understand," he finally said. "I don't feel sick. This was just supposed to be a routine check-up. I just felt a little tired and thought I could get something to pep me up."

Matt didn't take long to answer. This was not the first time he had to tell someone he was dying. It was never easy. But today was by far the hardest. Tom wasn't just a long time patient, Tom was a dear friend. They had been through so much together; school, marriage, children, golf—it was all part of the history they shared together.

"I understand," Matt managed, as he slowly sat down in the chair next to Tom. He gently put his hand on his old friend's shoulder and fought back the tears. "I wish I was wrong. You can't imagine how bad I feel." He paused for a few moments gathering his thoughts. "I want you to know that I'll be there for you and your family every step of the way."

Tom looked at his physician friend and managed a narrow smile. "What happens now?"

Matt gave a heavy sigh and answered, "Well, I'll write you a prescription. You'll take it everyday for a couple of weeks. You'll be off it for a week, and then, you'll need to come in for a weekly infusion of a follow up drug. You'll take that for ten weeks and then be off it for two while we monitor your progress. Our hope is that we can slow this thing down. As best as we know, the upside is, if there is an upside, there will be absolutely no pain. You'll gradually get more and more fatigued and feel the need to sleep more and more. Eventually you simply won't wake up. You'll maintain both your dignity and your basic mental capabilities throughout the entire sickness."

"Tom, because we're good friends, I know that you would feel awkward about asking for a second opinion. So I've taken the liberty to arrange that for you." Matt handed him a slip of paper with a name and number on it. "This is the name of a doctor I know who specializes in this type of disease. He's a friend of mine at Duke University Hospital, and he's good. I'll call and make sure they can see you as early as tomorrow."

The words sunk in slowly as Tom continued to stare off in disbelief. Eventually Tom broke the silence. "You know, you go to school, and you get an education. You work hard your entire life, and you do your best to provide for your family on every level. And somehow it still comes down to this. It just doesn't seem fair."

"It's not fair," Matt agreed. "And I know it doesn't make sense. I'm not going to pretend that this isn't hard, or that it won't be a struggle. But I will promise you that I will do everything possible from a medical standpoint to help you through this."

"Thanks, Matt," Tom forced. "I know that I can count on you. You've always been a good friend, and I appreciate that. I guess what I've got to do next is find a way to talk to Marcie and the kids about all this. That may be my biggest challenge."

The two grasped a firm handshake and hugged. Then two sets of eyes poured forth the tears that only strong friends could share.

The ride home was endless. Tom's brain was flooded with hundreds of thoughts, thoughts that he didn't want to have. He tried his best not to let his mind wander off in various scenarios, but he couldn't help it. He never visited the idea of physical pain. Matt assured him that there would be none. The pain he thought about was completely relational. His family meant the world to him, and he would give almost anything to spare them the grief he was sure they would experience. As the miles clicked by, he tried not to focus on the situation but with little success. At one point, he even thought about the irony of the entire story. Here he was, a salesman for one of the largest pharmaceutical companies in the United States, and he didn't have a remedy for the disease he had. He chuckled ever so slightly as he thought, *It's kind of like a distributor of bottled water dying from dehydration.*

Tom sat in his parked car for what seemed like hours. He was struggling with the words he would share with Marcie when he entered the house. He had run through more than a dozen scenarios but none of them seemed adequate. He knew there would be plenty of tears and hugs and that together they would face the children. *Oh, the children,* Tom thought, as a new set of tears and anguish advanced. *They're so young and so fragile. No kid should ever be faced with this. It isn't natural.* Tom reflected on each of the three children that he adored. *They're not even teenagers. They won't know how to handle it. They need me. This is not the way it's supposed to be.* All these thoughts and more flooded Tom's heart in an unrelenting succession. Finally, all the anger Tom felt jumped from his voice. Pounding the steering wheel he shouted as loudly as he could, "It's not fair! It's just not fair! I've been a good man. I've been a good husband and father. God, why are you doing this to me and my family?" Then he exploded with the sobs of a man without hope.

After gathering himself, Tom popped the door open and stepped out onto the sidewalk of their well kempt property. He was proud of the house they had built. It was everything they had always wanted in a home. Tom loved doing yard work, and his efforts in keeping the yard up were obvious to others. Tom looked at the yard and slowly shook his head knowing that this was no longer a priority. As he grabbed the railing leading up the steps, he felt the peeling paint on the iron rail and reflected on how many times he was going to get to the chore of repainting. Another thing falling off the 'to do' list, he mused.

Marcie cried without hesitation. Together they held each other and let the tears stream down their faces without embarrassment or interruption. But in the end, she handled it the way Tom secretly knew she would. She was always a kind, but strong woman. As they say, she had her act together. That's probably what attracted Tom to her in the first place. They had been married for 16 better-than-average years. They had had their moments of struggle from personality issues, to finances, to schedules, and agendas. But all in all, it was a very good marriage.

From the moment Tom saw her he pursued her. Their eyes first met in college during a football game. Marcie was a cheerleader, and Tom was, well, a student. He loved football and never missed a home game even though the play of the team warranted time better spent elsewhere. Marcie was a year behind Tom, but her strong personality and mature nature more than made up for the slight age difference. She was petite and athletic and quick to turn the head of any male with a pulse on campus. They formally met through a mutual friend after a less than stellar game. Marcie had more than her share of offers for dates, so Tom was pleasantly surprised when she accepted his offer of pizza on a Friday night. From that first date forward the path was cut leading to the altar. Now here they were, sixteen years and three kids later facing a challenge big enough for any five couples.

If this disease ran its predicted course, Tom would gradually lose his grip on life and Marcie and the kids would be forced to slowly and helplessly watch the man they loved so much slip away forever. Marcie would have to let go of the only man she had truly loved and the kids would be losing their daddy—the man who made them a family.

"How are we gonna tell the kids?" Marcie finally asked wiping her eyes and nose with an overly worn tissue.

"I don't really know." Tom countered. "But I do know that we've got to tell them soon. We've got to give them time to process all this. And we've got to give them the freedom to process it their own way. Matt gave me the name of a doctor friend at Duke Medical, and he's calling him to pave the way for a visit. I'd like to go tomorrow while the kids are at school." Marcie agreed and suggested ordering pizza and then sitting them down in the den to break the news.

Tom inhaled deeply and held his breath. Finally, he let the air escape slowly and nodded his head, "All right."

Tom and Marcie had great kids. They always believed that

good kids don't happen by accident. It takes a lot of investment both mentally and emotionally, as well as physically. They had paid their dues and, up to this point, were reaping the benefits. Madison was twelve and clearly the leader of the pack. She excelled in school and always seemed to be surrounded by friends. Like Marcie, she was a cheerleader, and captained her seventh grade squad. She was very close to her father and they shared a special bond built around their love for the outdoors. John, aged 10 was next in line. He was a rough-and-tumble kind on kid, who enjoyed playing football on the local recreation team. He wasn't greatly gifted athletically, but Tom and Marcie knew that his involvement was good for his ego as well as his social status. He was as close to Marcie as Madison was to Tom. Eight-year-old Matty rounded out the team. He was all engine and no rudder. He functioned as the family entertainer with his quick and explosive smile. He carried a toughness about him that often overshadowed his tender heart. He was always sympathetic toward others and had a great attraction to animals. Marcie labeled him an *M & M kid*, noting that he had a hard shell on the outside but was soft and sweet on the inside.

FRIDAY MARCH 7

The couple found themselves in Durham sitting in an examination room with Tom having more blood drawn. They held onto the hope that Matt's lab had made a mistake. It happens. Tom felt too good for it not to be an error. Although he had never been told he was dying before, and therefore lacked any comparison, he was sure that a dying man couldn't feel this way.

They left the clinic with the assurance that they would know the results within twenty-four hours. They rode home more on hope than on the wheels of their car.

Tom knew what it was to have hope. He was always optimistic. His life was built on hope. He also knew what it was like to be disappointed. He had faced that before. As they cruised down I-85, his mind drifted back to a day when he was just eleven years old. He was in little league try-outs. He had played in the minor leagues his first two years and was in the "international league" the previous year. This was his year to play in the majors. He practiced hard with his buddies and felt sure he was in position for the promotion. During try-outs he was pumped. What he lacked in size and speed, he made up for in enthusiasm. He struck out twice but hit three balls into the outfield—two on the fly, and one down the third base line. On defense, he stopped everything that came his way except for one ball that somehow squirted through his legs. Still he knew, at least he hoped, that he had done enough things well to warrant the attention of the coaches drafting for the big leagues.

Notification day came. As the phone calls went out he waited. A buddy of his called and two came by to share their good news with him. Tommy waited with all the anxiety of a first time father in a maternity ward. As the day dragged on, the silence of the phone grew louder. Half of him wanted to leave the house and occupy his mind with play. The other half dared not wander for fear that he would miss the call to glory and another boy would take his place.

It was late afternoon when the phone sprang to life. Tommy had it up before the second ring. He pulled it to his face and said "hello" before the receiver reached his mouth. Disappointment hit his ears. It was Mr. McDowell. He was a good guy and a good coach. But he coached an international team, not the majors. Tommy did his best to hide his disappointment, but his heart was broken. His last year in little league and he would be playing for an international team. Life couldn't get any worse than this.

Tom's mind flitted from there to the eighth grade science fair. He had done a good job. Unlike so many of the other students, whose parents *helped them* he had done his own work. His initial plan was to build a working volcano in hopes that the special effects would dazzle the judges. But volcanoes, even working ones, were old hat, so he abandoned that plan for another one.

He settled on a beaver lodge and dam. He did his research, gathered his supplies, and spent his time building a large replica of one of natures most industrious animals. He garnered a full sheet of plywood from the garage and used twigs to build the dam and lodge. He painted the water area blue and covered it with a piece of thick glass he rescued from a forgotten pane in his grandfather's barn. He built the lodge up and cut a cross section allowing viewers to see the tunnel and living quarters. He even had a family of beavers made of clay with one of them working on the dam, two in the lodge, and one in the tunnel complete with a branch in his mouth. Above the display was a colorful and neatly typed explanation of everything anyone wanted to know about beavers. A masterpiece! No doubt! Tommy was a sure bet to win, and everyone knew it—at least everyone related to him.

That night, he went to bed with all the confidence of an inside trader. He had even mentally cleared a place on the shelf for the trophy and prepared a few comments to be offered during the awards presentation.

Morning crept in too slowly. His dad slowly drove the truck to the school with the spectacular piece in the back. They placed it in a prominent spot in the gym and waited for the judges.

Three hours later, disappointment hit Tommy's chest like the fist of a heavyweight fighter. *Fourth place! Impossible!* He got beat out by a hovercraft, a remote underwater camera, and of all things, an active volcano complete with red lava-like ooze.

Tommy walked home that day more alone than he had ever been in his life. He left the small plastic trophy he had *won* in his locker. It wasn't fair! They must have been blind. He did his entire project without any help. That night he surrendered to sleep struggling to fight the tears that eighth graders aren't supposed to shed.

Yes, Tom knew what it was like to have hope shattered. Yes, he knew the pain of having a sure thing evaporate into an unsure thing. But he also had his share of realized dreams. In fact, the fruition of his hopes far outweighed the disappointments in his life. He hoped he would be accepted at Brentley and he was. His junior year, he hoped to make the Dean's list, and he did. And the best one of all, in the fall of his senior year, he hoped Marcie would go out with him, and she did, giving him a life that birthed every reason to live with hope.

So they traveled the interstate full of fear and clinging to hope like a man at sea waiting to be rescued.

That night, after the kids finished off the last of the pizza, Marcie ushered the kids into the living room. Tom and Marcie couldn't eat, and were secretly agonizing over the possible reaction of the children. The kids seemed ambivalent due to the fact that *town hall meetings* had been a part of their upbringing and could be called to announce anything from *we need more help around the house* to *we're all going on a cruise this year.*

Madison and John sat comfortably on the couch while Matty dove into the overstuffed chair. Tom and Marcie sat next to each other on the footrest facing the children. Each drew a breath and Tom began to speak. "I'm afraid I have some very bad news for you. I've been to the Doctor's yesterday, and he told me that my test results came back, and they show that I've got a very rare disease. They can treat it, and maybe slow it down, but they can't cure it."

Madison broke in, "What are you saying? That you're

sick? What does that mean?"

"Well," Tom began again, "the doctor said that because there is no cure, that I may have as little as six weeks to live." There. He had said it. And it was every bit as hard as he imagined it would be. The look on the kid's faces cut into his heart like a knife. He wished his words were different, but like so many things in his life from this point forward, he had little choice.

The house was as silent as the day it was built. All three of the young ones sat there desperately trying to force their brains to process all that they had just heard. Tom and Marcie waited, resisting the temptation to break the silence with more information.

Finally, John spoke up through a crackling voice, "What do we do now?"

"Your father and I have talked this out a good bit before you came home" Marcie said. "We're just as shocked as you are about this whole thing. We haven't worked it out and a lot of what we're going to do we'll figure out as we go along."

"That's right," Tom inserted. We're really not sure what happens next. But we do know three things we are going to do. We're going to stay together as a family. We've always been close but this could be something that will make us all a little closer. We're going to enjoy each other's company and make as many memories as we can. And we're going to pray. We've always counted on our faith to get us through tough times, and this is another one."

Marcie slid her one hand in Tom's and squeezed his shoulder with the other. John and Matty each left their perches and came over and hugged their Dad.

Madison's reaction was quite different. "That's it? That's the plan?" she questioned as she stood up and her eyes reddened, filling with tears. "Get close, have some fun and pray?" Maybe I'm missing something. But in six weeks I'm gonna lose my father. There's no cure. There's no hope. What am I supposed to pray for? Why should I talk to God when He's about to take away my daddy?" With that she raced across the room and down the hall to her bedroom slamming the door behind her.

Tom and Marcie just looked at each other and held onto the boys who by now had stopped fighting the tears. Tom's cheeks expanded as he slowly let out a lung full of air. He patted Marcie's knee and quietly said, "I'll give her a little time and then go speak to her."

A soft knock was heard on Madison's door. Tom didn't wait to be invited in. He knew there would be no answer. He also knew that Madison would be on her bed with her face in the pillow. Tom's mind reeled back to other occasions when he was called upon to intervene in the crises of a young and tender heart: a friend who moved away, a teacher who made an unfair comment, a boy who was just plain mean, all these and more, Tom handled one at a time in a sensitive and levelheaded way. But this was different. This was oh, so different. No amount of experience or information gathering could ever prepare him for this mountain that he must help his sweet twelve-year-old girl to climb.

Tom slowly walked to the side of the bed and sat in the place that he had grown so accustomed to. He stroked his daughter's back and sat next to her listening to her unbroken sobs. Somehow she looked so small. She seemed so brittle. Madison was a fighter. She was fearless. She was a go-getter. She succeeded at everything she tried. And now she was faced with losing something that was so precious to her, her father. Tom and Madison were extremely close, unusually close. They had a bond between them that went way beyond their mutual love of the outdoors. They were knit at the heart. Together they would face this thing that would threaten the very fabric of their relationship.

"Honey, I'm so sorry," Tom began. "Believe me, this isn't easy for me either. In case you've forgotten, I'm the one who's dying." Tom's minor stab at humor didn't faze Madison. She kept crying, not wanting to face him but knowing that she must.

Slowly, she turned her torso towards him. "Daddy, I'm so sorry. I love you so much," she cried punctuating her feelings with her embrace and wiping her wet face with her hand. "My whole life, I knew that you would always be there for me. I've daydreamed about you dancing with me and us going hiking up to Kane's Canyon. I can't tell you how many times I've thought about my wedding and having you walk me down the aisle. I've even thought about what a great grandpa you would be and how much my kids would love seeing you. And now I have to deal with the fact that you're not going to be there. It's too much! It's not right! It's not fair!"

Tom's face was now covered in fresh tears. He held his little girl as tight as he safely could. There was no way that she could know that he too was dealing with thoughts of all the things he wanted to do, but now would never realize.

"I know it hurts," Tom said. "I'm hurting too. We're all hurting. But we're just gonna have to trust God on this one like all the other things we've been through. I trusted God with your life when you were first born, and now you're gonna have to trust Him with mine." Tom referred to Madison's birth when there were complications and she had to stay in intensive care for over a week. They didn't know whether or not they would be bringing their little one home.

"I know," Madison finally said. "I know you're right. And I want to trust God. It's just gonna take me some time to dial this whole thing in."

"I understand," Tom said as he held her and kissed her gently on the forehead.

Surprisingly, Tom slept well. He and Marcie had stayed up

late alternately talking and crying. They had prayed and drifted off to sleep amid ideas, plans, and regrets. They affirmed their love for one another and their commitment to stay together through it all.

SATURDAY, MARCH 8

Tom was up early as was often the case. He possessed the complimentary traits of being an early riser as well as a meticulous planner. He spent most of the night thinking of all the things he needed to do in the remaining weeks of his life. This didn't seem like reality. It seemed like he was being forced to live the hypothetical question, *what would you do if you only had six weeks to live?*

After a light breakfast, Tom sat down at the table and began writing. Since it was Saturday, he anticipated his family sleeping in. This would give him the welcomed opportunity to put down some of the ideas that had been churning in his head. He had a fresh yellow notepad with numbers down the left margin. Two years ago, during the Christmas holiday he had asked each of the kids to write down and hand in what he later called *the big ten.* He encouraged them to dream big and tell him the top 10 things they wanted to do with him or the family. He told them that they needed to list big things that would be great adventures and experiences. The plan called for Tom to compile all their ideas and then, as the years unwound, for them to click off each of the ideas as opportunities presented themselves. Dutifully, each of them came back with their list of desires.

Hawaii, New York City, the Grand Canyon, and a hot air balloon ride were all included in the lists. Tom knew that time would not allow them to complete thirty items. So his task was to prioritize each of the requests and then set into motion plans to make them come true.

Tom had done a good job in preparing his financial future. They were by no means a wealthy family, but his income, coupled with their investments and retirement, enabled them to make some of their plans come to fruition immediately. Tom reviewed each of the lists and noted the commonalities among the lists. Hawaii was on each of their lists as was New York City. California was on two of their lists along with hang gliding. Tom saw that although they weren't in a position to do each item, there might be a way to cram in several of their desires in one big trip. Within an hour, Tom had a plan. The pages were covered with stars, cross outs, arrows, and lines. Another sheet carried dates, locations, and activities. Before long, Tom possessed what he considered a logistical masterpiece.

Not long after Tom finished making plans, Marcie entered the kitchen and hugged him from behind. Glancing down at the sheets of paper on the table she smiled and quietly said, "I figured."

Tom patted her arm and responded, "I guess a leopard never changes his spots." The children filed in shortly afterward, still dressed in their bedclothes. In succession, they kissed and hugged their father and found a place to sit around the table while Marcie poured some orange juice for each of them. Each of the children had fallen asleep amid tears springing from the pain in their hearts. And each of them awoke rolling the crust from their eyes and struggling to re-grasp the news of the previous evening. It was evident that Madison's tears had already returned that morning but she did her best to keep her emotions in check.

Tom broke the silence forcing himself to sound upbeat. "Listen guys, I'm sorry we had to share that news with you last night. I know it isn't easy for any of us. I wish things were different. I really do. But unless the clinic tells us something different, this is what we have to deal with."

"Now you know that our faith has always carried us through. God still loves us and God is still in control. Remember how we taught you Hebrews 13:5? Let's see it." Each of the children held up their hand with fingers outstretched. Tom led the way assigning a word to each of his fingers while pointing to them. The children each followed along. "I will never leave you. Remember what we told you to do when life gets tough?" Each of the kids closed their hand and held their fist over their heart. "That's right!" Tom smiled. "We also taught you to always, always have a plan and to never, never give up. Wait 'til you see this!" he said as he leafed back to the first page of his lap pad.

With all the excitement of a family at Christmas, they gathered around Tom while he mapped out a strategy for a family trip that would exceed any they had imagined. The idea of missing school couldn't hold a candle to all they would experience. The New York City leg included a Broadway show, the Empire State Building, The Statue of Liberty, and several other sites. The California stage involved the redwood forest and the San Francisco bay area. The Hawaii destination would offer scuba diving, hang gliding, a hot air balloon ride, swimming with the dolphins, as well as nearly a dozen other activities. The trip home gave them time in southern California and places like Hollywood, Beverly Hills, the San Diego Zoo, Universal Studios, along with several other points of interest. When the excursions were tallied, the number of *big ten* activities they would experience came to nineteen. Following this, would be the return to North Carolina and all that was involved with the future they silently understood they would have to face.

Two hours later, the clinic in Durham called only to confirm the findings of Matt's office. Tom and Marcie weren't completely surprised but were still disappointed and hurt. They held each other and fought back tears feeling the weight that replaced the small hope they held onto. They guarded their feelings against being overly pressed with optimism. They knew it was a long shot but they still held loosely to it like a high school girl waiting for that special boy to call all the while knowing he won't.

The next two days passed in a flash as weekends often do. But the following two days at school and work dragged on like a bad voice performing a solo. Tom gave the news to his boss in person over breakfast. Because he dealt in outside sales, he called those whom he was closest to in the company. They all processed it in disbelief. Tuesday found him packing up his office and finishing the details of their trip.

Marcie spent her time informing her supervisor that she would be gone for an indeterminate amount of time. She relayed that she would understand if they decided to fill her spot at the university where she had worked in the accounting department for the last six years. Before work, Marcie had made a trip to each of the schools to explain the situation. The children were each given notes to deliver to their teachers. Before they left, they would be assigned work to be completed during their trip. Everyone felt bad for them, but nobody really understood. How could they?

WEDNESDAY, MARCH 12

As the wheels of the plane left the ground, all members of the Redden family knew they were in for the trip of their lives. The moment they touched down in New York, even young Matty understood the meaning of the term "carpe diem."

Between the shows of Broadway, the immensity of the redwoods, the beauty of the Hawaiian Islands, and the captivating experience of Universal studios, each member of the family breathed in all life had to offer. Each day found them exploring, looking, and learning. Nights were spent laughing, talking, and listening. They concluded each night with prayer, and appreciation for the events of the day and each rested with the certainty that this is how family life is supposed to be done.

Fourteen days later they pulled into their driveway in North Carolina pleasantly exhausted from the experience. Tom had noticed a definitive drop in his energy level but combated that with an extra dose of caffeine mixed with intermittent bursts of adrenalin. The goal of squeezing every second out of life became more and more urgent.

THURSDAY, MARCH 27

Marcie spent the morning on the computer. She was traversing the various web sites trying to find out something, anything about the disease that had found a home in Tom's body. She could hardly pronounce "leukopapliomegitus," much less understand where it came from and what it did. After over two hours of searching she came up with only seven sites that gave her a hint about the disease. Basically she found that it was a type of cancer that migrated from the spinal fluid and attacked the red blood cells at an alarming rate. When she finally wheeled away from the desk she understood that in fact there was very little information out there and very little that could be done. All of the treatments were still in the experimental stage, and no conclusive progress had been made to stop it. It was a disease without cause or prevention.

For over fifteen minutes Marcie stared at the floor. She couldn't claim to be thinking of anything. She was mostly just trying to take in the concept of her husband being terminally ill with no hope of a cure. It was all so surreal. This was something that happened to other families. This was something that other people had to deal with. This is what their family prayed about for other people but not for them. Marcie tipped her head back, took a deep breath and wiped away a tear. Even though she knew very little about what was going on inside of her husband's body, she knew Tom well enough to know what was going on inside his heart. If there was anything that characterized her husband, it was that he was a planner and a fighter. She knew, without a doubt, that her job in this episode of their lives together, was to be strong for her husband. Sitting in the black swivel chair in the study, she resolved that no matter where this disease took them, she would stay by her husband's side and do everything she could to help him through it.

FRIDAY, MARCH 28

Tom and Marcie arrived at the clinic for further blood work. Everyone was curious about the progression of this enigmatic disease. Tom had been faithfully taking his medication while secretly hoping that it was an unknown cure. Matt made arrangements to be there and greeted both Tom and Marcie with the hug of a friend. His love for both of them was never in doubt. Marcie held Tom's hand as a nurse drew blood from his arm. Tom called the blood "high test" and commented on how normal it looked. The nurse was pleasant and lighthearted, revealing that she probably didn't know the gravity of the situation.

"We'll have a better idea of what's happening when we compare this sample to earlier ones," Matt informed them. "You're being placed in a study group and depending on what we find out, we may be able to make some headway in combating the disease that others may get."

Tom was all about helping others. It was a way of life for him. He had taught Sunday school, coached John's little league team, volunteered for special events at each of the kids' schools, and served on the local board of directors for the Fellowship of Christian Athletes. Everyone knew that when there was a need, they could always call on Tom and he would make arrangements to be there to lend a helping hand. His steady example and thoughtful insight made him a welcomed member of any group. Now he was in a different position of assisting. Now he was helping out with more than his back or brains. This time he was giving a piece of his life so that others would have a better chance at theirs.

Tom and Marcie left the clinic and headed into town for lunch with some friends. They walked into their favorite restaurant where they met Jim and Teresa. The couples hugged, holding onto each other longer than normal. The embrace communicated more than friendship. It signaled a deep care and affection and let Tom and Marcie know that they were in the presence of friends who would always be there for them. They had known each other for over twelve years. Tom remembered where they had first met. Tom and Jim were brought together by a mutual friend. The Reddens were planning on adding a playroom onto their home and needed the help of an architect. Jim fit the bill and did an excellent job not only in drawing what they needed but adding his personal input as well. Every time Tom saw the room's specialized inset bookshelves, he thought of Jim.

Jim had a rare sincerity about him that easily endeared him to people. He was one of those people who actually waited for an answer when he asked how you were. When you talked to him, he always looked you in the eye and communicated clearly he valued what you had to say. Marcie and Teresa hit it off right away. They were so much alike in their personalities. They were both fun loving and Teresa had a sense of humor and quick wit that brought laughter to any group. Except for differences in their hair color, they even looked alike. Jim and Tom even kidded them about being twins and plotting some adventurous scheme to overtake the men.

After they were seated, Jim and Teresa wanted to know all the details of their trip. They listened as Tom and Marcie shared all about the family excursion. Predictably, Jim wanted to know how Tom was doing. He asked about Marcie and specifically inquired about how each of the kids was handling things. Tom told them about the blood work and the medication along with the treatment plans. "You know, the strange thing is, aside from feeling a little tired during the day and really tired at night, I don't feel sick. I'm not hurting anywhere." Then shaking his head and shrugging his shoulders, he added, "I guess I should be thankful for that." They each gave an affirming nod at Tom's ironic conclusion. The conversation quickly moved to other things and the four affirmed their love for each other while making plans to get together soon.

The kids came home from school at the usual time. John informed everyone that he was starving as if that was new information. John was always hungry. Marcie fed him a good breakfast and packed him a complete lunch. There never seemed to be enough food in the house for this growing boy. Although he did very well in each subject, John hated school. He often talked about inventing a "brain pill" that would eliminate the need to go to school. He and Tom would regularly daydream about what they would do with all the money that idea would generate.

Matty's love for school matched John's hatred of it. He had a really good teacher and always had good friends around him. He adjusted very well to new situations and was quick to get on his schoolwork, seeing it as a barrier to his playtime.

Madison came in talking. School was important to her mostly because it provided her an opportunity to be with all her friends. She was a good student but kept a safe distance from being labeled a bookworm. She loved to read and she enjoyed writing poetry and songs, but saw no need of studying certain types of math she was convinced she would never use. Today she talked to her Mom and Dad more than usual. She told them about the latest relationships that were forming, the plans she and her friends had for the weekend, and how unfair it was for her English teacher to dismiss one of the boys for being out of his seat. She went on and on about the new car one of her friend's parents bought and even questioned where they got the money. She talked about how wrong slavery was and how she didn't want to do the upcoming assignment in English. Tom and Marcie let her go like a fisherman letting a bass take the line. They smiled at each other recalling the importance of letting her share her heart.

Tom's mother and father had been deceased for over eight years, but Marcie's parents were very much alive. Her father had done very well in the computer technology industry, placing them in a position to be comfortable during their retirement years. They spent half the year in Florida and the summers in the mountains of North Carolina. They had been home for two days when they got the call from Marcie. After their share of tears, the decision was made for them to come and spend a few days with the Reddens and then be there as the situation dictated. Being only a few hours away made it much more convenient to come when called. That's the way they had always done it. They had been good parents and in-laws, being very supportive but not intrusive. They had learned the fine art of exposing rather than imposing.

The children loved them dearly and Marcie had always had a close relationship with her parents. Tom got along especially well with Henry. He knew Henry could never replace his dad but felt like he was as good a substitute father as one could hope for. Henry was always there with words of encouragement or information. His analytical bent had come in handy when Tom and Marcie were laying out the plans for their house. Tom considered him more than a father-in-law. He saw him as a friend. Elaine was the type of Mom that was always prepared. If anyone had ever carried a servant's heart, Elaine did. She was the consummate caregiver. From cookies and milk to a portable sewing kit, she was quick to step in whenever she was called on. She adored Tom, which made Marcie somewhat jealous. Marcie would often accuse her mother of taking Tom's side whenever there was a disagreement between Marcie and him. Whenever Marcie would bring this up in a conversation with friends, Tom would often chide her by saying, "Don't be mad at her because she's right," or "Your Mom can't help it if she's plagued by good judgment." These comments were usually met by a rolling of her eyes or a soft jab from an elbow.

TUESDAY, APRIL 1

Today was the day Marcie's parents would be arriving. After lunch, Tom looked out the window and spied their car coming up the short driveway. He timed their reach for the doorbell with the swinging of the front door while at the same time yelling to Marcie, "Honey, I think the clearing house sweepstakes people are here!" When the door opened completely, he yelled, "Oh, it's just your parents. But maybe they brought some money."

The three gave an unhindered embrace with Marcie's voice behind them, "May I come to this love feast?"

"You better," Elaine said as the circle widened and Marcie joined them in a warm hug.

The bags were all moved in, and the two couples sat drinking coffee and talking about the great trip the family had enjoyed. As expected, Henry brought some gravity to the conversation by saying, "Tom and Marcie, there can't be any doubt that we love you and the kids. If there is anything we can do for you, just let us know. We'll be just a phone call away."

Through glistening eyes, Tom and Marcie thanked them, and they all gently guided the conversation in another direction.

When the kids bounced in from school, the celebration of family began. Hugs and kisses exploded in abundance followed by the dispensing of the usual Floridian gifts. Each of them including Tom and Marcie was given a t-shirt. Ironically, Tom's displayed a wrinkled old man with the words, "I'm still kickin' but I'm not raising any dust." Tom showed it off by holding it up to his chest and smiled, "How appropriate!"

Henry noted, "We debated about giving you that, but we knew you would pout if you didn't get a gift."

"And don't ever forget that!" Tom said laughing. Each of the children was given a couple other trinkets evoking kisses and hugs of appreciation. Tom and Marcie had quietly felt that her parents spoiled the kids a little too much but in light of the situation, they didn't let it cross their minds.

WEDNESDAY, APRIL 2

Tom kept his usual standing appointment with an old friend. Tom and Perry had been accountability partners for over fourteen years. They had been meeting in one of about four restaurants for lunch with amazing consistency. They frequented these four establishments so often that the owners as well as all the waitresses knew them by face if not by name. They enjoyed the greetings and even kidded about being welcomed like Norm on "Cheers." The entrance for each of the men today would be the same as always. A slight smile found its way across Tom's face as he reflected on his relationship with his buddy. Beyond their faith and their love for their families, there were more aspects of their lives that would have driven them apart than the strong bond that held them together.

Perry was athletic. Tom was not. Perry was from up north. Tom grew up in the south. Perry was black, while Tom was white. Perry was more aggressive while Tom tended to be laid back. Still, their friendship had brought them closer than any two men tended to be. They had vacationed together, played golf together, and had served on some of the same community organizations together. Their families had spent a great deal of time with each other, and the two of them used the occasions to bridge racial gaps and to teach their children to look beyond skin color.

Perry's wife Laura was a beautiful woman both inside and out. She was average in height and thin and possessed a smile that could light up any room. She was a highly charged creative woman with enough energy for two people. Those were assets that came in handy as she home-schooled their three children. They had been married for about the same amount of time as Tom and Marcie, and the two girls got along very well feeding off of each other's energy and united in their efforts to coral their two men. It was not uncommon for one of the women to call the other with the news, "guess what our husbands are planning now?"

As Tom sat waiting for Perry, he reflected back on all the times they had shared. He revisited innumerable conversations they had had ranging anywhere from money, to kids, to marriage, to church, and sexuality. They had communicated freely both their dreams and fears and always came away with the feeling that they were both better men for the experience. Tom remembered how he had talked Perry into taking his two boys with Tom's sons on a camping trip. They had paddled out to an island in the center of a large lake. Perry's flimsy reasons for not going included bears, snakes and the Klan. Finally, he relented, and the men and boys had a memorable time.

At one point in their relationship they purchased a home in need of repair. Their goal was to finish it quickly and "quick turn" it for "big money." They had found a house that fit the bill and started working on it almost immediately. And, with almost as much speed, they learned that they were in over their heads. The repairs cost more, took longer, and required more work than they anticipated. Though silent, their female counterparts often stood at a distance shaking their heads and wearing that "boys will be boys" look. When the project was completed and the home was sold, they each netted out a little less than three hundred dollars. The two men left the attorney's office, and crossed the street to the car.

Looking over the roof of the car, Tom said, "Perry, do you know what this experience makes us?"

"No" Perry countered, "but I'm sure you're gonna tell me."

Tom held up an index finger and said, "Number one, we're officially real estate developers." Then holding up a second finger he said, "And number two, we're 'hundredaires."

Perry rolled his eyes saying, "If I don't laugh, I'll cry."

Tom said, "Well, if we have a choice, let's laugh!" Then he gave out a big yell and said sarcastically, "Man, I feel good! Come on. Lunch is on me. And you can have anything you want on that hot dog!" They both slid into the car secretly understanding that they were both wiser men having experienced the joint venture.

On another occasion, they came up with the idea of kidnapping their wives. They planned out their strategy like a couple of school kids making plans to build a tree fort. They spent two of their meetings making sure all the details were in place. Each man had specific tasks to do and the two kept checking on each other's progress by phone. When it was time to go, everything worked like a well-oiled machine. Well, almost everything. Each man had made arrangements for their parents to arrive while the kids were in school. They had rented out a three-bedroom cabin in the mountains complete with four wheelers and a lake. After the repair of a flat tire, a return trip to a restaurant for Tom's wallet, a stop for some items that Laura had forgotten, and a quick run through the grocery store for supplies, they arrived at the cabin in time to enjoy a wonderful sunset over some flavored coffee and a side-splitting game of cards.

Both men agreed that part of the enjoyment of the trip was the surprise and excitement they saw on their wives' faces. Everything had been done secretly including the destination and who would be joining them. Marcie figured out who was coming when she and Tom had gotten about three miles from Perry and Laura's. Laura guessed that they were going to the mountains when they turned a particular way on the interstate. None of them guessed how much fun and laughter they all would enjoy. The entire weekend was a home run, and the men enjoyed the satisfaction of having done a good job in executing their plans.

Countless thoughts roamed the recesses of Tom's mind. He finally settled on how he and Perry first met. On a particular Friday night, Tom and Marcie pulled into the parking lot of the local video store. They had been out to dinner with plans of going to the movies. Having scanned the cinema's offerings, they opted to see what was on the shelves. The parking lot was full, giving them the feeling that the choices in the store would be slim. They found a spot toward the back of the building and headed inside.

After twenty minutes of browsing the shelves, they narrowed down their choices to two. One was an old title, and the other looked kind of silly but was under the new releases. They debated between the two as they stood on the end of a fairly long line. Finally they decided on the older movie, and Tom left to return the other selection. No sooner had Tom left, than Marcie remembered that she had left another DVD in the car brought along specifically for return. She called to Tom, but he couldn't hear her. She left the line and made a quick exit toward the car.

As she neared her car, she pulled out her keys. She never saw him. And she never saw them. When she reached for the door she finally noticed a man out of the corner of her eye. The young man had stepped between the two cars and was leaning against the trunk. He wore baggy pants and a cap on sideways. His mouth carried a toothpick and around his neck were three gold chains. One of the chains ironically held a cross. Then she saw two more men to her right one of which had jumped up and was sitting on the hood. "Well, what do we have here?" the man in the back said. "You think you got a little time for us?"

The moment he began speaking she was aware of two things. They were big, and she was in trouble. "Please" was all her voice could manage.

As two of the men stepped toward her, she heard another voice. "Mary!" a fourth man said. "Mary, we thought you were still inside. John's waitin' for ya. Come on! We're ready to check out." As he brushed passed the two men, he gently took hold of Marcie's arm. Instantly Marcie knew what was going on. Turning slightly to the trio, he said, "How ya doin' fellas?" He nodded toward them and escorted Marcie away while he continued to talk. "John wanted to get a drama but I told him that you'd rather see a comedy. Me, I don't care. I just know…" his words trailed off as Marcie replayed the scene in her mind. Out of the corner of her eye she could see the three young men disappear into the night. When they neared the door to the store, Marcie's eyes began to fill with tears. The reality of what had just happened and what could have happened was beginning to settle in. This stranger had just rescued her from who knows what. It was very possible that he saved her life.

When they entered the store, Tom found her immediately. "What happened?" Tom said seeing the shaken look on her face.

The man spoke up. "My name's Perry" he said extending his hand.

Tom grabbed his hand knowing that the man had done something to help his wife.

"I was going out to my car when I saw these guys moving in on your wife. We changed their plans."

Marcie couldn't hold back the tears. She buried her head in Tom's coat and began to cry. Hearing the commotion, the manager of the store came over. A security guard stepped through the door and headed around the back of the building. As Perry talked to the manager, Marcie relayed to Tom the details of the confrontation through breaks in her sobs.

When the manager had finished talking with Perry, Tom approached him with his hand extended. "My name's Tom. I don't know how to thank you." Perry shook his hand, and the two began a relationship that would go way passed that night and beyond anything the two could have anticipated.

Perry entered the restaurant donning his traditional smile, and the two men gave their usual hug. They had already talked by phone and cried over Tom's news. Perry and his family had processed the situation with an equal amount of tears, ending their family night with prayers for Tom and his family.

Ever since they started meeting, Tom and Perry's relationship was always on a unique level. They learned to be open and honest with each other and could quickly take a conversation from the superficial level to great depths. They could easily go from, "How's your job?" to "What do you think a man's greatest family responsibility is?" Today would be no different.

Over the years so much of their dialogue was sporadic and unplanned. They just started talking, and the information and emotions just poured out. They liked it that way. They never knew what they were going to talk about and rarely came in with an agenda. Today was a little different. Perry had processed this thought in his head, long before he met with

Tom. He didn't know how he was going to bring up the topic, but he was sure that it was an area that the two men had to visit. "In a very strange way, you've been given a unique gift," Perry said.

The look on Tom's face invited Perry to explain. Perry leaned forward in his chair. "Tom, even though we don't talk about it and try to avoid thinking about it, every man knows deep down inside that he's going to die. None of us knows how or when, but we do know that nobody gets out of here alive."

Now it was Tom's turn to lean in. His body language said *you have all of my attention.*

Perry continued, "You see, not only do you know how it's gonna happen, but you also have a pretty good idea when it's gonna happen. And because you have a handle on each of these things, you can make more definitive plans than the rest of us."

The words sunk in deep. Tom turned them over and over in his mind. After a moment he looked at his old friend and said, "If I have a choice, I think I'd rather win the lottery." Both men smiled, knowing that the attempt at humor was a simple defense mechanism. "So tell me, what should I do?"

Perry drew in a deep breath. "I dunno. But think about this. You are now in a unique position to answer the question everybody asks. "What should you do with the rest of your life?" "I think I know you really well. We've been through so much together, and I can easily say that I've never had a friend like you. I am so thankful for you and all that we've done together. But knowing you like I do, I believe you need to spend your time with the three greatest priorities of your life: God, your family, and people. Your faith will sustain you, and the people in your life will encourage you. Listen. You're getting ready to meet one of your priorities and at the same time, you're getting ready to leave the other two. Your job is to prepare to do each of those things equally well."

As usual, the two men had delved to communication depths that few relationships allow. They continued to visit and dive to various levels. Before either of them glanced up at the wall clock, two hours had passed, and Perry needed to head back to work. As they hugged their good-byes, certain words kept echoing in Tom's mind, *gift, plan, God, family, people.*

Across town and an hour later, Marcie met in a small coffee shop with three of her closest friends. The ladies had been meeting together for over four years and had developed a closeness that allowed them to share their struggles as well as their victories. Donna, who constantly struggled with her weight, but compensated by a heightened sense of humor, was the first to arrive. One couldn't label her obese, though she often referred to herself as such, but she did carry more than her share of weight. The ladies continued to support her and encourage her particularly in the area of her self-esteem. Gena walked in with Marcie. Of the four women, they had been friends the longest, having met as volunteers at the local Christmas resource center.

Gena was tall and attractive and possessed a steadiness about her that endeared her to friends and strangers alike. Gena was from New York, and she was a giver. She had the directness about her often seen in northerners, but she buffered that with the type of kindness rarely seen in anybody. She and her husband Roger had done particularly well in the family real estate business, putting them in a position to meet the needs of others as they came to their attention. They lived modestly, having the unique understanding of how much is enough and had made a conscious decision to share as much of their assets as they could. They had even forgone family vacations to help someone else. They started a foundation whose sole purpose was to provide the needed educational materials for inner city elementary aged students.

As usual, Veronica arrived last. Veronica always arrived last. She always wore a watch, but it made little difference.

She was just one of those people who was chronologically challenged. Jokes about her being late for her own funeral were common. The girls often considered telling her they would meet a half hour earlier than the agreed upon time just so that she would be there close to the correct time. For her birthday, the gang gave her several gag gifts regarding this particular flaw. She got a wrist sized sun dial and a calendar with the exact times of their scheduled meetings already penciled in. She also received an engraved plaque with the number of the international time center written five times. There was even a large wind up alarm clock that made insulting remarks in order to motivate you into starting your day. She took the ribbing well, and didn't hesitate to return the volleys. She often told the girls, "If I wasn't so important to each of you, it wouldn't matter if I was late. Among the tribe there was always a lot of laughter balanced with the study they had committed themselves to.

Each woman there knew without speaking that today would be a unique day. Marcie had called each of them shortly after she had a chance to process Tom's news herself. As they spent time on the phone, each of the girls had shared thoughts with the others. One thing they knew: Marcie needed them and they would be there for their dear friend.

As Veronica finally slid into the booth, there was a sort of tangible uneasiness among them, centering around Marcie and Tom's situation. Their love for Marcie spilled out on Tom much the same as a parent's love drifts over to the friends of their child. They tried to counter the awkwardness with small talk but quickly understood the futility. The group slowly grew quiet, and Marcie's eyes welled up in tears as she broke the silence. "What am I gonna do? I'm not ready for this! I never dreamed that life would be like this." The tears came quickly now as Marcie put her hands to her face. Sitting next to Marcie, Gena put her arm around her friend, and each of the others reached out and placed their hands on her shoulders.

Finally, Gena spoke. "We love you girl, and we're going to be there for you."

After a brief pause, Marcie said, "I know. And you girls don't know how much you mean to me. Thank you so much for being my friends." The entire group unsuccessfully fought back the tears that spoke of their love for Marcie.

In short order, the tears had run their course, and Donna broke in. "Let me tell you what we need to do. We each need to go up to the counter and order one of the desserts that we try to resist every week. Then we need to come back here and begin to plan a big party."

"A party?" Veronica asked.

"Yeah, a party." Donna said with her typical animated face complete with the smile that displayed almost all of her teeth. "Let's have a 'celebrate life' party!"

Gena jumped in and gave Marcie's shoulder an extra squeeze, "That's a great idea! You know how many friends you and Tom have. We'll rent out the Moose Lodge and invite a whole mess of people. It'll give you and Tom a chance to see all the people who love you both so much." Then the New York personality she usually kept in check came bursting out. Using her hands to punctuate her words and speaking loudly in a heavy northern accent, she said, "And Marcie, if you and Tom don't like it, den yuz don't gotta come. But we're gonna have a party anyhow." The entire booth, including Marcie broke out in laughter. Then the planning began. Before they left, they had a tentative date, the choice of two bands, three DJs, a partial menu, some ideas for decorations, and a long list of guests to invite. The ensuing weeks would solidify the rest of the plans the ladies made.

At each of the children's schools, word had gotten out about the kids' dad. The teachers had all been gathered together and informed by the respective principals. They wanted to be prepared with support and encouragement along with sensitivity toward the children in their charge. After just a few days most of the whispering and quiet talk had died down, and the students treated the Redden kids the way they always had. The friends closest to the children were especially helpful and let each of them know how sorry they were. Three friends of Madison's volunteered to help any way they could and in the coming days, solidified their friendship by giving her more hugs and attention than usual.

In Matty's school the kids moved to the level of patronization. Any close calls in gym class always went Matty's way. When there was any disagreement at lunch, Matty was always right. Even his teacher found herself going easy on him whenever she graded anything that he turned in.

John experienced similar grace. Most of his classmates knew him to be a chocolate addict. Their assessment was accurate. Tom and Marcie kidded him about writing in Milton Hershey for President. On John's first day back from vacation he found a large colorful note on his locker that said, "We're with you big John!!!!!!" The moment he opened his locker, various types of chocolate bars spilled out, covering his feet. At home, he lay on his bed and counted the candy bars like Ebenezer Scrooge counted his coins. Before dinner, he bounced into the kitchen and announced to the family, "427. I have 427 candy bars. I'm rich!"

Tom looked up from the paper and said, "You know, John, if you divide those up with the rest of us, then we could each have enough for about 80 days."

"And if I don't," John countered, sitting down heavily in his seat and smiling a boyish grin, "I'll have enough for myself for 427 days." The family laughed knowing that it was John's nature to be generous and anticipating plenty of chocolate for a long time. Matty didn't laugh so hard. He just wasn't too sure he could count on his big brother's benevolence but resisted playing the "Mom, make him share" card.

Tom slowly warmed to the idea of a party. He was outgoing and energetic and he loved people, but he wasn't the kind of guy who liked a lot of attention. With a few of Marcie's hugs and some kisses on his neck, he finally said, "O.K. Let's party!" Each of the children thought a *celebrate life* party was a great idea. Not needing an explanation, they all understood the purpose and plan of the party. Like Tom and Marcie they enjoyed any excuse to get together with friends for a celebration. Within minutes, they each had a guest list of their own.

TUESDAY, APRIL 8

Tom knew that there would be plenty of days where sleep was all that he desired. This was not one of them. Not being able to sleep, he got up before 5:00 with his mind reeling in random thought. He went to his study, spent some time praying and reading his Bible, and started planning. Planning came naturally to him and details were simply an extension of who he was. But in a very real way, he surprised himself about his enthusiasm for the task at hand. From his previous meeting with Perry, he had settled a few things in his mind. This morning he would take care of one of them. Tom was going to plan what few people ever do. He was going to write out the details of his own funeral. This seemed so strange to Tom. A great deal of him still couldn't believe his body was dying. Except for the fact that he felt a noticeable drop in his energy, and relatively early in the evening he had to fight to stay awake, he felt fine. This entire scenario seemed unreal.

Within three and a half hours, the task at hand was complete. Tom had taken care of everything. The music, the speakers, the soloists, the processional, and recessional, pallbearers, even the funeral home that would walk Marcie through the entire process were covered. No detail was left out. He had even written a long letter to be read to those in attendance. For a few minutes, he toyed with the notion of building his own casket out of a pine box but dismissed the idea as too morbid. He slowly shook his head as he considered how having their Daddy's casket lying in a corner of the shop would make his kids feel.

There were five other items to be inserted in the large envelope Tom would give to Marcie later that day. One was a list of all their assets along with the numbers of all the people who could help her along the financial trail. These people included their life insurance agent, their investment broker, their financial councilor, and the law firm that would handle all the legal affairs.

Tom had planned their financial future well. He knew the importance of living below ones means and now experienced an eerie kind of satisfaction knowing that Marcie and the children would receive the benefits of his discipline. Between the life insurance pay out, and their investments, there would be ample money to pay off the house, send each of the children to college, and leave enough for Marcie to live off of the reinvested dividends.

Another item to be added to the envelope was a list, complete with phone numbers of all the people to be notified in the end. Though Marcie was quite capable of keeping several plates spinning at one time, this was one more detail she would not have to worry about. He even had people listed at the top of the page suggesting them to take care of the calling.

Next, Tom put in his own obituary. Another detail Marcie would not have to deal with. This was not an easy piece to compose. *What do you say about yourself? What's important? How can you let friends know about you without sounding narcisstic?* Tom reflected and wrote, reflected and wrote, and then rewrote all he had written before coming up with a few highlights he felt compelled to include. He listed his family, his schooling, his church and community involvement, as well as a couple of honors he'd received. Tom couldn't honestly list any of the things that men long for. He never wrote a book, he never saved someone's life, he never traveled extensively. His was just the fairly simple life of a man who loved his Lord, and his family, and was ready to jump in and help his fellow man any way he could. For just a few moments he smiled as he thought how sad it is to live a few decades and summarize your entire life in just a few short paragraphs.

The next two items to be included were bathed in tears. Tom wrote a letter to his children as well as his wife of sixteen years. Each of the letters was first written by hand and then typed. He had to stop several times to wipe his eyes before continuing. There was so much to say and precious little time to say it. After soaking six tissues and laboring over the note pad for a half hour, Tom had encapsulated his thoughts for his children:

To my sweet, sweet children,

Time does not allow me to tell you all the things I want to share with you. I love you all so much and count myself blessed to have been your father. I know this is a very difficult time for you. I know you have shed many tears and still have more to shed. But please don't feel sorry for me. Even as you read these words, I am with my Lord and enjoying all the glories of heaven.

You will get through this. I promise you that. Please stay close to each other and your Mom. You're going to need the help and encouragement that only a family can give. Don't ever forget all the great times we had filled with laughter and excitement and how we grew both as individuals and as a family.

Stay close to the Lord. He is the great comforter and will always be there for you. Do not be bitter because he chose to bless me before he blessed you. Do not lose your faith. His plans are always right, He is always good, He is always loving.

Life is full of uncertainties. No matter what you go through and no matter where life takes you, be certain of this, I will always love you, and I will always be proud of you, and I will see you again.

Until the Lord brings us together again—All my love,

Daddy

Tom didn't think it was possible, but it seemed like the tears over the letter he wrote to Marcie flowed even more forcefully. They had been through so much together. She had given him three terrific kids, turned a house into a home, and enabled him to grow into everything he was. *What do you say to a woman who has shared so much of your life with you? How can you possibly put your feelings on paper?* Marcie had been a great wife for Tom. Her personality and interests complemented his like a hand in a glove. They just fit together. It just felt right, like the feeling you get when you put on a warm pair of old jeans or a ball cap that has become your favorite. She was so much more than a wife. She was a dear friend. What words would suffice to relay all Tom's heart contained? It seemed an impossible task, but he would do his best.

To Marcie—the Love of My Life,

If a man could write out all the things he looked for in a wife, he would still come up short of all that you are to me. I can clearly say the last sixteen years have been the best years of my life. I could not have asked the Lord to send me a better wife! The love you have given me, the sacrifices you have made, and the ways you have cared for me go way beyond the bounds of marriage.

What we both are experiencing is not a parting. This is simply a short interruption of the love we share. Night has fallen in our lives, but the sun will come up again shortly. The love that I have for you is strong enough to cross the line between heaven and earth, and I long for the day that I will see you again. Until then, please know that you are the only woman that I have ever loved and that I will wait for your arrival and meet you inside the eastern gate of the kingdom of God.

I love you with my whole heart!

Eternally Yours,

Tom

Tom addressed two envelopes, one to his wife, and one to his kids. He took each of the notes and placed them in the separate envelopes, and then inserted them into the larger envelope.

He had so much more to say and do, but life, as he would soon experience, is painfully short. His dreams, his desires, his love, his past and future were each sealed in the envelope that he would present to Marcie later that morning over coffee. Tom knew that Marcie would be o.k. (at least from a financial standpoint). She was mature and possessed a deep faith. He was, however, concerned about the children. *They're so young,* he thought. *Especially Matty.* He was uncertain whether or not his youngest son really understood that in a short period of time he would lose his Daddy. *Children need a father. They need a dad who will always be there to give them stability and wisdom,* he pondered. *Who's going to be there to attend their games and to help them figure out life? Who will give them the strength and security that only a man can give his family?*

Tom turned these thoughts over and over again in his head. He knew Marcie was smart. In fact, in many ways, her brain outdistanced his. He knew she would continue to pour her life into theirs, and she would be there to give them the guidance and support that they needed. She had always done that. Marcie was a well-organized, caring, and loving woman. She always displayed a patient and nurturing heart. She filled so many gaps where Tom was lacking. But Tom also understood that while no man can fill the role of a woman in the life of a child, there is no woman who could stand in the place of a man in the life of that same child. The wiring is different and each brings a unique ingredient to the mix. Tom knew he still had so much more to give and so much more to share with these precious people in his charge. How could he possibly inject into his children all that they needed to know about life in just a few short weeks?

Then it hit him. When Tom was in college, he began collecting quotes. Some of the quotes were by famous people while others were written by men and women who the world would label unknown. He even had written many quotes himself. But each of the quotes had something to do with a positive outlook on life or at least called for the reader to stop and consider what was said. Some were amusing while others could be used to shape a person's individual philosophy. Tom had hundreds of what he called *notable quotables*. He even kept a file on his desktop that he would periodically add to. When he came across a quote, either by ear or by eye, he would jot it down and put it in a stack that he kept in a desk drawer in his study. Then when he could find the time, he sat down and updated his categorized collection.

Tom turned in his chair to face his computer. A quick move of the mouse brought the screen to life. A small movement of the cursor along with a left click of the mouse, sent hundreds of quotes to his eyes. Tom scrolled down the page stopping several times to digest a particular quote. Mark Twain had written, "The preacher didn't charge nothin' for his preachin,' and it was worth it too." Yogi Berra said, "When you come to a fork in the road, take it." These were filed under the title "humorous." The larger file of course, held thoughts that ran deeper in their message. Margaret Thatcher wrote, "No one would remember the Good Samaritan if he only had good intentions." From Rich Beach came, "Affliction colors your life, but you get to chose the colors." From the pen of Tom Landry he read, "Mental toughness is the ability to do your best under maximum pressure." All these and so many more were a part of Tom's life. They were a part of his outlook, his philosophy, and they did so much to shape his personality and help him face so many difficult days. His hope was that they would help the children to develop a positive outlook on life and to see the great possibilities life offered.

Each year, as summer came to a close, Tom would sit down at his desk and pull out some of his favorite quotes. He pasted these quotes to another page and then printed them out. He made sure there were at least forty because these were to be shared each week with his kids. Then every Monday morning, Marcie would slip one in each of the kids' backpacks and they would read them sometime during the day. Several times, great discussions would start over dinner as one of the kids had a question about it. Most times though, the quotes were not mentioned. Still, Tom knew that the wheels were turning and the information was getting in. So often Tom would see Marcie jot down a quote that had particularly appealed to her. He knew it wouldn't be long before he found it on their bathroom mirror or that Marcie would be sharing it with her girlfriends at the coffee shop. Tom always smiled the smile of a man when he knows he's done a good thing.

As Tom scanned the hundreds of quotes before him, his eyes were searching for one in particular. It was one that he had come across while still in college but one he had shared with dozens of people throughout the years. Tom bounced through various categories and then settled on it. It was under the category "Life" and was actually an adaptation from something Benjamin Franklin had penned. It simply said, "If you don't want to be forgotten shortly after you die, either write something worth reading, or do something worth writing about." That was it! That was what Tom was looking for!

As Tom reflected on his life, he knew that he had done nothing in the past, nor did he possess the time in the future to do anything someone would find worthy of writing. But perhaps he could write something worth reading. A friend of his, who had written several books, shared with him, "A good writer needs something to say, some way to say it, and someone to say it to." Tom had something to say. The way to say it was staring back at him in the form of a monitor. And he knew, if he knew anything, he had some people he needed to say it to. The three people fell into the category of his children and he had so much he wanted to tell Madison, John, and Matty. His own wheels were turning now.

The door to Tom's study opened slowly. It was Marcie. Being sensitive not to startle him, she quietly opened the door. She never knew if Tom was praying, reading a book, or playing a video game John had downloaded on his computer.

She gave him a firm hug from behind, and Tom swiveled in his chair and pulled Marcie to his lap. "Couldn't sleep again last night?"

"Nope. But I got a lot of things done. Let's get some coffee. I've got something I want to share with you." How many times had Marcie heard those words? Tom was always sharing with her. Normally he was somewhat laid back, even predictable, but he often got excited and became quite animated in his delivery. His inspiration often came from something that he read, an idea he had, or something from his childhood. Marcie always welcomed those encounters but gained a new appreciation for them in light of their unknown future.

As Tom sat down across from Marcie, she slid a cup of coffee his way. When she took her place opposite him, he countered her move by sliding the large envelope her way. She took it with one hand while Tom stroked the back of her free hand. "What's this?"

"This is what I've been working on since early this morning. I think it's going to make things easier for you and the kids." She didn't open the large envelope before her. Her eyes started to gloss over in tears, but she managed to hold them in check. She really didn't want to go where she knew the conversation was heading.

Finally, she found herself asking, "What do you mean?" Tom continued to caress the back of her hand.

"Honey, I know this has not been easy. And you've done a great job holding up so far. I can't tell you how much I appreciate you and how proud I am of you. But I also know that things are going to get harder. When it's finally…." Tom hesitated. He really didn't want to finish the sentence, not the way he knew he had to anyway. He took an audible breath and continued, "When it's finally over, I don't want you burdened with trying to figure out everything on a practical level. I think this will make everything a little easier. That's all."

Marcie didn't respond. Marcie couldn't respond. Her own defense mechanism moved her into a busy schedule. Her days were always full of activity, and lately, they had kept her from focusing on what she didn't want to face. But now with *the envelope* before her, she was pushed into looking at the future in full frame. Tom continued, "This envelope has all the information you need regarding our finances. It's full of numbers, and accounts and the names of all the people you need to contact. It also has a list of all the people you should contact to let them know what's going on." Tom did not want to go on. He knew he was hurting Marcie but knew equally well he had to fill her in on the rest of the contents. He lowered his voice and raced through his next sentence. "I even wrote out my obituary and how I want my funeral to go."

Marcie looked at him in disbelief and, with a tear escaping from her eye, could only muster the word, "Tom!" Tom got up from his seat. He went around the table and knelt next to Marcie. He brushed the single tear from her face and held her firmly in his arms. He was now fighting his own tears.

In a few moments, he began again. "I know it's not easy to deal with this, but it's just something I have to do. Maybe this is more for me than for you. I'm sure there's some head shrink somewhere who would label it therapy. Anyway, I also wrote a note to you and one to the kids. I'm gonna put all this stuff in the safe, so it'll be there when you need it."

A wave of relief came over Tom's soul. In his mind's eye, he never imagined it would be so hard to communicate all this to Marcie. His biggest fear was in hurting her. He had faced that fear and was glad it was over. Marcie never opened the envelope. They both stood up and embraced. Marcie rested her face against Tom's chest. It felt so good. It felt so necessary to be held. She never wanted to be free of the comfort of his arms. A moment later Marcie said, "Tom Redden, you have got to be the most organized man on the planet. But when you get to heaven, promise me you won't try to change too many things right away." They both gave into a quiet laugh and concluded their time alone with a passionate kiss.

As if on cue, all three of the kids bounded into the kitchen. There never seemed to be a lack of energy or noise in the Redden household. Declarations like, "I'm starving!" "I'm gonna be late!" and "Did you wash my sweatshirt?" were as common as ants at a picnic, but a whole lot louder. After a quick swipe at a hastily fixed breakfast and a kiss for both Mom and Dad, the trio grabbed their books and exploded out the door. Marcie's plans included shopping for a few items for that night's party and going to the gym for a perfunctory workout. Tom was scheduled to pick up the dry cleaning and then meet over brunch with two friends from Sunday school.

FRIDAY, APRIL 11

What a party!! Marcie and her team had gone way above and beyond the call of duty and had even surprised themselves with how well everything had come together. "Celebrate life" posters and banners were everywhere. The amount of food that people brought was only surpassed by the variety. A large poster board was set up so that everyone attending could tack up pictures of themselves enjoying life. There were vacation pictures, graduation pictures, newborn baby pictures, and wedding photographs. The party was scheduled to begin at 7:00, but people started showing up at 6:30. The early arrivals were immediately put to work and by 7:15 the lodge was packed with friends and family. They came from work, church, the neighborhood, and other social circles. A welcomed surprise was that several of Tom and Marcie's friends from college showed up. Some came as far as 200 miles away. The food, the laughter, the music, the noise, all combined to send a clear message that life was to be celebrated. A large table was littered with well wishing cards thoughtfully selected with the most personal of notes included.

Fortunately for Tom, he had forced himself to take a nap right after his brunch meeting as well as in the late afternoon. He felt great and was highly energized by the great showing of friends and family. The last of the guests left around 11:30, and Tom and Marcie headed home and to bed right after praying over each of their children. A wave of exhaustion hit Tom. He was remarking to Marcie how good it felt to have so many friends. He noted how wealthy he felt that night and started to complete his thought but drifted off in mid sentence.

SATURDAY, APRIL 12

Tom spent the first three hours of that morning reading each card that was given. Each card brought a memory of a person they had grown to know and love. Each card also caused Tom to be thankful for such great friends. There were cards from high school friends, college friends, work associates, friends at church, and even cards Marcie saved from some who couldn't attend the party but mailed them on ahead. All counted, there were well over two hundred. There were some cards, however, that made Tom pause, and travel back in time to a chapter or episode of their lives together. Tom found himself reading the card, seeing who signed it and drifting to a place in time where they had traversed together. There was Wayne, a high school buddy. He and Tom, along with Wayne's father, fixed up a go-cart with twin engines and a live axle. They had purchased it cheaply and spent every spare moment they had, sanding, painting, and repairing it. In the end, they gained a fine piece of machinery along with a tremendous education. They raced it a good bit before blowing an engine and selling it for more than they had invested in it.

There was his cousin Frank's card. Tom smiled widely as he thought of the great memories they had shared. The card said something that an outsider would never understand. Tom knew immediately what Frank was communicating. It simply said, "Bombs away!!!" and "SULFUR RULES!!!" Tom and Frank were not only cousins, but close childhood friends for several years before Frank's family moved away. Frank was the adventurous type, lingering on the brink of mischievous. Together they camped, built tree forts, fished, explored caves, and launched rockets.

One sunny summer morning, Frank bounded into Tom's room with the most amazing of discoveries. He had found a book that explained how gunpowder was made. "With this formula, we can make our own bombs," he said with all the excitement of a boy who found buried treasure. Both boys were giddy with excitement as they suggested all the things they could blow up and the great noise they could make. Without delay, the two boys began rounding up the necessary materials, and by the end of the week, they were in position to make their way to the woods to try out this new find.

Not far from one of their hideouts, they made a small pile with the powder, connected a long tail for safety, got behind a tree, and struck a match. They touched the match to the powder trail and watched as the flame quickly moved along the dirt. Not knowing what to expect next, they lay down behind the tree and covered their ears. No sound could be heard, but an amazingly large ball of white smoke, coupled with the distinct smell of sulfur assaulted their senses. Knowing that it would not be long before someone in town saw the smoke, the boys abandoned their position and raced toward home. When they slowed to a quick walk, they each promised secrecy if questioned, and made plans to meet the next day.

As fortune would have it, no one in town caught on to their mischief, and the next day found them at the hideout, ready for another plan. This time, Tom brought a half roll of duct tape, and Frank brought the inside of a paper towel roll and several packs of firecrackers. They taped one end of the cardboard cylinder closed and filled the rest of it up with the powder they kept in a jar. Then, they took several firecrackers and removed the fuses from them. They spliced the fuses, ending up with one fuse about eight inches long. Then they taped the other end of the tube shut and used the remaining tape to reinforce the walls of the cylinder.

They set the bomb down on the other side of a tree, lit the fuse and hid behind a large rock about twenty feet away. Again, they covered their ears and waited. There was a muffled thud followed by a loud hissing sound that lasted about three seconds. The boys peered around the rock to find the area around the tree engulfed in flames. This time there was no escaping the sight of the neighbors. They had spied the pillar of smoke and turned their attention to the cause. In short order, there were three men joining the boys in stamping out the flames. Water was brought from the nearby creek, and soon the fire was under control and extinguished. The day's events concluded with both sets of parents extracting a promise that the boys would never do something like that again. It was a clear three days before the soreness in Tom's hind parts showed any sign of relief and two weeks before his body saw any freedom from the confines of the yard.

Another episode found Tom and Frank snorkeling in the fishing area of Shepherd Lake. Each time they surfaced they possessed hooks, weights, and lures left by those whose lines had broken from a snag. Before they were marched out of the area by the ranger, they were able to completely stock each of their tackle boxes with enough supplies to see them through five summers of fishing.

Tom returned the card to the envelope and opened another. This one was from Doug Pinnock. Doug was Tom's tenth-grade biology teacher. Doug was a talented teacher and well equipped to deal with the students in his care. He took a particular interest in Tom and was instrumental in Tom's selection of colleges. He was one of those teachers that students naturally turn to for advice and direction. After college, the two men had lost touch but restarted their friendship a few years later. His card was filled with encouragement and contained the words, "So glad the Lord brought our paths together." Tom smiled and shook his head when he read the words that he so often heard his teacher say, "The early bird gets the worm, but the second mouse gets the cheese."

The next card made Tom think more on the philosophical side of life. It said, "You will never know how much your friendship has meant to me. Thanks for your influence. I will never forget you!" It was from Bob. Tom met Bob when they were freshmen in college. Though they majored in business together, Bob became a lawyer and lived a little less than two hours away. He and Tom met during orientation and hit it off immediately. Throughout their college years they studied together, went to parties together, visited each other's homes on weekends, and double dated. If fact, it was Bob who introduced Tom to Marcie.

Tom always admired Bob. When Bob had decided on a direction, he stuck with it. He was not one to bail out at the first hint of trouble. This paid off in school as well as in his law practice. He started out slowly with just a secretary and a small office. Over the years, his practice grew, until he now had five associates, two paralegals, and three secretaries. Still, he kept balanced business hours making sure he took the time to meet the needs of his wife and four boys.

Bob was a good man and good things seemed to come to him. He enjoyed dabbling in real estate and came upon a find that really paid off. He went to a land auction where a one-acre parcel of land was to be sold. The location was good and Bob thought that he could hold the property for a short while and then sell it for a profit. He bid on the parcel and won, paying below market value for it. The deed was turned over to him and he held onto it for two years.

When the market was right for him to sell it, he had it surveyed again and found that there was a mistake on the original survey. The survey labeled it a 1.08 acre piece that was nearly rectangle in shape. When the new survey came back, it was found to be 10.8 acres. Bob had purchased a parcel that was ten times as big as he thought. Without delay, he sold the property to a developer realizing a profit of over $200,000!

True to his nature, he bought an entire playground set for the local elementary school and used some of the money to match an endowment chair challenge at Brently College. Some of the money was added to his children's college fund and the rest was used for a vacation trip to Hawaii for his family. Not one thing that Bob did surprised Tom or any of the others who knew him.

When they were freshmen, though they weren't roommates, Tom and Bob lived on the same floor and spent a lot of time together. It was Tom who came up with the idea of a Turkish bath. They removed the closet doors from Tom's room, turned them sideways across the opening of the hall shower, stopped up the drains, and let the water flow. In less than an hour, they were joined by several of the other fellows diving into the large bath area. The next day, both young men were summoned to the Dean's office where a tongue lashing, along with a lesson on structural engineering were forcefully given. They managed to talk their way out of being suspended.

One night created an unforgettable memory in their lives. It happened during their junior year. They had been studying in the library and decided to take a break and get a milk shake at the campus eatery. While wandering back, they passed by one of the academic buildings called Gladesdale. Along with academic classrooms, Gladesdale housed the campus bell tower. Each hour, the huge base sounding bell informed all those within earshot of the time. Bob remarked to Tom how he wondered what it would be like to get into the bell tower. In less than a moment's time, they found themselves staring at the trap door leading to the tower. They noted the small lock and knew that their path had come to an end. Intending to establish the hopelessness of the situation, Bob pulled on the lock only to find the rusty hasp give way.

Both of the young men worked their way to the top and spent a few minutes gazing at the campus below. They marveled at the size of the bell and ran their fingers along the edge of the mass of metal. Tom noted that it was only a few minutes before the hour and that they would do well not to be in the tower when she sounded off. When they made a move toward the stairwell, the shine of a security guard's flashlight alerted them to the fact that they were in trouble. Because he was an elderly gentleman, and at the bottom of the stairs, they knew they had a few moments to think. Secretly, they wondered if he had seen them enter through the side door. They knew there was only one way down. They knew they were trapped. Without words they understood that although standing on the trap door would prevent him from entering the tower, the broken lock would alert him to their presence.

Their only hope was to find a place to hide. But there was no place to go. "The bell!" they whispered together. In less time than it took to come up with the idea, they were climbing inside the bell and scampering up the clapper. Using the bulb end of the clapper as a step, they remained motionless and quiet as they waited for the old man to enter. They watched his light go around the room and hoped against all hope that he wouldn't look up. It seemed like an eternity, but finally he retreated. The boys saw his light fade through the cracks in the trap door and knew they were safe. Well, not completely. It was almost nine o'clock and in less than a minute, the grand lady of the tower was set to make her announcement. They continued to watch the light traverse the winding stairwell knowing they dare not leave the room prematurely. They heard the grinding of the gears as the clapper was raised to one side of the bell. Then whoosh—it came cascading against the inside of the mass of steel. Bob and Tom each lay curled up in a ball with their hands pressed tightly against their ears. The sound was still deafening and they could feel the percussion against their chest with each ensuing swing. When they knew there was no escape, they each decided to count the number of gongs to determine how long it would be before they experienced relief. After the first few gongs, they lost count and moved into the mode of endurance.

When the last hit came, they slowly uncurled and came to a seated position. Neither boy spoke. They just slowly made their way down the stairs wondering if the other was feeling the buzzing in his ears as well. They glanced around outside and exited the building of torment. As they walked back to the library, Tom put his arm around Bob's shoulder and said much too loudly, "Well, now you know what it's like inside the tower." Both young men laughed the kind of nervous laugh when you know that you've just sidestepped a major accident.

Sometimes Brentley College didn't offer much of a social life on the weekends, so the students were left to create their own form of entertainment. Young men possessing free time is rarely a formula for good things. On one such Saturday night, Tom came up with an idea that had others talking for days. Somehow, they had sequestered a long piece of surgical tubing from the biology department. They quadrupled the length of tubing and secured each end to the hinges of a couple of open doors at one end of the dormitory hall.

Next, they covered the tile floor of their hallway with soapy water. Two young men were assigned the task of pulling the tubing while another, clad in pre-soaped shorts, sat down on the floor with his back against the tubing. When ready, the tubing was released and the young academic was launched down the hall. The goal was to see who could slide the farthest. Like little boys in line for the ice cream man, each fellow vied for position naming whom they were to follow.

All went well until it was Edward's turn. Edward was an undersized computer whiz from the outskirts of Memphis. Try as he might, he never seemed to fit in. He was awkward in a social sense and never included in the normal events of campus life. But as Tom and Bob looked over the growing crowd of young men, there was Edward wearing his shorts and waiting his turn. When his moment came, Edward sat dutifully in place and gave the thumbs up sign for readiness. No one is quite sure what happened next. Maybe the "pullers" pulled a little harder. Maybe his lack of size had something to do with it. But whatever the reason, Edward was launched down the hall much faster than any previous projectile. He sailed passed the previous record and slammed into the radiator at the far end of the hall. Everyone fell down laughing until they realized that Edward was not getting up. Upon inspection they found him to be out cold. He was taken by ambulance to the hospital where he spent the night and was released the next day with a grade three concussion.

After that incident, the boys on the hall were a little kinder to Edward partly out of pity and party out of respect because he never revealed the truth of what happened that night. The story he circulated was an unfortunate fall down the steps in the dorm. Maybe it was because of the accident or maybe it was because he never let on to what really happened, but for whatever reason, Edward developed some close ties with a few of the boys and even swelled a bit whenever the subject was brought up.

Tom and Bob's friendship continued to remain strong long after their college days. They were part of each other's wedding ceremony as well as participants in each other's parents' burial. They laughed together, they cried together, they played together and they grew together. They had traveled a lot of emotional miles side by side and were each a stronger man for the trip.

Tom whispered another thankful prayer as he slipped the card back into its envelope. He finished looking at all the cards and gathered them up in a stack—so many friends, so many memories, so many blessings. The former night's feeling of wealth, overwhelmed him, and he promised himself he would visit some more of the memories in the near future.

Late, very late, that Saturday morning, the family had plans to join two other families for lunch and then a couple of games of lazar tag. It had been a long time since the family had played, and they were all looking forward to it. John wound up with a welt on his cheek when he rounded a corner and ran directly into another player's gun. He was no worse for the wear and a small ice pack seemed to take the swelling down in short order. Tom commented about how dangerous it was to play with women because the *Mercy gene* was overridden by the taste of blood. Marcie simultaneously hugged him and labeled him a sore loser. After the weapons were abandoned, the crowd headed for the movie theatre. Popcorn and sodas were handed out, and then the group settled down in their seats to escape into the world of fantasy. Before heading home, the Reddens stopped for pizza and ice cream. Normally Tom would be guilt ridden over spending so much money in one evening, but he was quickly settling in his mind how unimportant money really was.

SUNDAY, APRIL 13

Like most Sunday mornings, the Reddens were found in Sunday school and church. As they settled into their pew, Tom reviewed the worship schedule. Marcie, being more musically inclined, really looked forward to the worship music. Tom was much more interested in the message. Pastor Cobbs was fairly new to the congregation. This was the fifth church he had served in, and the people seemed to take to him readily. He wasn't flamboyant, but he possessed an intellect demonstrating that each of his messages was assembled under the discipline of a lot of study. Tom always left with a deeper understanding of the message. Today's sermon was titled, "A Life that Matters." *This should be a good one,* Tom thought as he turned the bulletin over and glanced at the prayer requests.

Instantly, Tom's eyes fell to a name, his name, among all the others in need of prayer. Tom inhaled deeply and held it in for a moment. He slowly exhaled as he processed what that meant. He had never been on their prayer list. He had never been on any prayer list. He wanted to feel like it was a typo, but he knew beyond a shadow of doubt that his name belonged there among the rest. Without a word, Tom nudged Marcie and tilted the bulletin toward her with the nail of his thumb marking the spot. Marcie gave a half smile and gentle nod. At the same time she felt so thankful that they belonged to a church that was so caring. She had no doubt that prayers would be lifted up for the entire family. She also had no doubt that those prayers would be deeply needed.

In the days to come, Tom found himself spending less and less time in front of the television and more and more time with family and friends. It's funny how life takes on new meaning when you realize how short it is. It's kind of like the strange feeling you get when you've heard so much from older people about how quickly time flies and then arrive at where you not only agree with them, but you actually experience it. Tom was there. Oh, how he wished he wasn't.

One night, Marcie had given Tom one of *the signals*. Every couple has signals. These were private words or gestures shared only between a couple that communicated to their spouse that they had a desire to be physically intimate. Both Tom and Marcie knew what their signals were. If Marcie lit a few candles, suggested to Tom that he needed to come to bed, or wore a particular nightgown, Tom knew a special time was in the making. Tom was much more overt and much more verbal. He would often give Marcie a hug and say something like, "How about getting together with me tonight?, How tired are you?" or "Could I interest you in some romance?" Sometimes their sessions were spontaneous, and sometimes they were routine. But nonetheless, Tom always, always looked forward to them.

MONDAY, APRIL 14

Tom lay in bed and allowed his head to remain deeply sunk in his pillow. He smiled slightly as he replayed the previous night's experience. He could hear Marcie breathing evenly and glanced over at the form of the woman he loved so dearly. For reasons he couldn't explain, his mind traveled back to a time when he could have easily pitched everything he now held so dear.

They were only a few years into their marriage, and Marcie was uncomfortably pregnant with their firstborn. Work was uncharacteristically difficult, and their home needed some substantial repairs leaving them with unexpected bills. Tom rarely traveled out of town, and his overnight trips each year could be counted on one hand. But because of an administration glitch, and the need for Tom to help a regional director with a new territory, he was asked to fly down and lend a hand. He didn't want to leave, but knew it was necessary. So nervously, he boarded a plane that carried him to Mobile. He had met Renee, the new regional director, several years earlier at one of the company's national events. She, like Tom, had been a company representative with her own territory. Renee was an attractive slender single woman with dark hair and a smile that had a way of putting people at ease. She was about two years older than Tom and not more than three inches shorter. Everything about her was professional. She looked and dressed the part of someone in management and displayed complete self-confidence in everything she did. Their paths had crossed in several company events, and they had been in meetings together, but that was clearly as far as their relationship had gone.

So it was more than a surprise for Tom to find himself seated across from Renee in the restaurant of the hotel where they were staying. They had spent the day traveling around the area and meeting with other representatives. When Tom pulled the rental car into the parking deck, Renee mentioned how hungry she was. Tom agreed, and Renee asked him if she could buy him dinner. Before Tom even thought about it, he found himself saying yes. He had just crossed a bridge and found himself unable to retreat. Tom was on foreign turf and felt uneasy.

Their communication at the table could be labeled professional with work maintaining center stage. Renee began to ask Tom about his home life, and Tom talked openly about the impending arrival of the baby. Renee shared how she had been married but never had any children. The conversation continued along these lines and seemed fairly harmless. When dinner was over, they both turned down the offer of dessert, and Renee paid the bill. As they walked toward the elevator Renee smiled at Tom and said, "I don't know what you've got planned for the rest of the evening, but you're welcome to come up and have a drink." Tom's mind was in high gear almost to the point of panic. He wasn't certain where she was leading and didn't want to misevaluate the message. He wrestled with the flattery of the offer and found himself wanting to say yes. Conversely, he knew he had no business being alone in private with a woman who was not his wife. He could hear the arguments for accepting the invitation and the benefits of enjoying himself in her company. *No one will know. You deserve this. What's one little drink gonna hurt?*

Tom didn't want to embarrass her by making her feel foolish. He liked her. He really did. But he had a strong sense of what was right and knew the only answer he could give would be no. As they reached the elevators, she pressed the button. "I appreciate the offer," he said "but I'm a little tired and have an early flight in the morning."

"Sure, I'm a little tired too," was all she countered with.

If dinner was uncomfortable, the elevator ride was

excruciating. Staring at the numbers, Tom wondered if they were riding in the slowest elevator in the city. Finally, the doors opened on his floor. He shook Renee's hand, wished her luck, and exited. When he felt the doors close behind him, he looked back at the elevator and slowly shook his head while breathing a nervous sigh of relief. The only thoughts that came to his head were, *Tom, that was really stupid.*

The words of his father appropriately spoke to his heart. "Every moth loves the flame. But the ones who fly too close always get burned." Another small shake of his head sealed his understanding of the truth of that comment.

As he pushed the key card into his door, he thought of an ethics professor he had in college. Ethics wasn't a required course for those majoring in business, but it should have been. The teacher's name was Dr. Davidson. He was phenomenal, and Tom really enjoyed the class, learning so many things he still applied. He was blunt in his delivery almost to the point of antagonism. That may have been one of the traits that attracted Tom to his style of teaching. What came to the surface of Tom's mind at this moment was a comment that Dr. Davidson had made one fall morning. He said, "Friends, don't think that for a few moments of bedroom pleasure, you can't sacrifice everything you hold dear in your life." That comment sunk deep in Tom's brain. He rarely thought of it but never forgot it. What really drove that comment home was when Tom learned over the summer that the professor had been dismissed due to his involvement with one of the female students.

In his room, Tom sat on the edge of the bed in self-condemnation. *How could he have let himself get into that situation? What might have happened to his relationship with Marcie? What would the future have been like?* Over and over he asked himself those questions never finding an answer that would let him escape the feeling of foolishness. Still, being a man of facts and bottom lines, he understood that nothing sinful had occurred. He had not betrayed Marcie and the vows he made to her.

He remembered being on a retreat in the mountains with a group of men from the church. They had an incredible time filled with hiking, studying, with plenty of food and laughter. The speaker for the weekend was tremendous. Tom couldn't remember his name, but he remembered so much of what he said. In one session, he instructed the men to, "make your decisions before the options present themselves. Decide what you will and will not do before emotions have a part in the formula." It all made so much sense. If you make decisions about what you will or won't do and develop that into a rule, then your head won't be clouded over by the emotions of the moment. You can walk the moral line without the danger of compromise, and you don't have to suffer the consequences of bad decisions.

Tom replayed the previous two hours. He had told Renee no at the elevator. That was a good choice. There was, without a doubt, a struggle but his deepest conviction had won out. Where he messed up was in accepting her dinner invitation in the first place. If he had said no to the first question, then the second question would never have come up. Tom fell back on the bed relieved that nothing had happened and resolved that nothing would. He reached for the remote as the phone rang. His fear that it might be Renee caused him to hesitate. He was determined not to see her tonight. He knew it would not be a good idea. As he picked up the phone, he was visibly relieved to hear the voice of Marcie. Three times during their conversation he found himself saying, "I sure do miss you," and "I can't wait to get home."

Tom looked again at Marcie. He realized anew how much he loved her. She was everything he needed and more. He often commented to his close friends that Marcie was evidence that God does have favorites, and he was at the top of the list. To save face and to score some possible points with their mates, those in the circle always countered with positive comments of their own. *It's been a good life,* was all Tom managed to think. He rolled over on his side, gave a sigh of gratification and dozed off again.

WEDNESDAY, APRIL 16

The afternoon mail brought a welcomed surprise. Tom and Marcie had filed a disability claim with their insurance company. They were uncertain how long it would take for everything to pass through all the proper channels, so they took care of all the paper work and let things run their course. That day they received the first of several checks that would help them during the next few months. They were so thankful they still had some income to take care of their current living expenses. This was yet another way they witnessed the benefits of planning ahead.

Marcie's ladies gathered again around the booth at the coffee shop. True to form, Veronica was late, Donna was jovial, Gena was encouraging, and Marcie was still wearing the mask that said, *everything's all right.* Without words, the girls knew that Marcie was struggling. They had communicated to each other the need to be supportive and had done several things to lift Marcie's spirits. Unbeknownst to the others, each of them had sent Marcie a card, letting her know how much they loved and appreciated her. They told her they would be there for her and invited her to lean on them whenever she needed. Marcie was so grateful for such good friends. She knew that in this fast-paced, self-seeking world, friends like these three were as rare as water on the moon.

Early on, in their relationship, one of the commitments the four friends had made was to reach out and try to make someone else's life better. So they targeted someone they all agreed could use some help or encouragement. They called it the "E assignment." "E" stood for encouragement. The plan was to find someone they all felt could use some form of encouragement. At the beginning of each month a person was mentioned along with a little bit of information about her circumstances. When the idea was brought up, the women cautioned each other about the possibility of this turning into a gossip session. They decided that only confirmed facts would be given and only enough information would be shared about the person to inform the group of the need at hand. There were two parts to the plan. The first part involved prayer. The ladies committed to pray each day for the individual chosen.

The second part involved a blessing. Each of the ladies agreed to fast during lunch on the day before the three of them would meet. Ironically, this was Donna's suggestion. The plan was that they would save the money they would normally spend on lunch and put their savings into a *blessing box* to be given in some form to the person they had selected. They agreed they would ordinarily spend about five dollars on lunch, so they each brought that much as a *blessing tax*. In this way, they understood they could give a real blessing to at least twelve people each year making a difference in the lives of the recipients. What they learned was that the blessing went to both the givers as well as the receivers. Sometimes the blessing was monetary. Sometimes the blessing was an actual gift to meet a specific need. As often as possible, the blessing was anonymous with only a note of encouragement attached.

They purchased prom tickets for the son of the woman who cleaned the building where Gena and Roger worked. They bought a gas card for a husband and wife when he was laid off. They gave school supplies to the son of a single mom. There were food cards, children's shoes, groceries, and books. They gave flowers, food, a school trip, and birthday party supplies. The women had as much fun deciding what they were going to give as they did in giving the gift.

One year, they supplemented their plan with a little extra to provide Christmas presents for the three children of a family whose father had recently died of cancer. The ladies were ecstatic as they bounced from store to store picking out everything they knew would bring a smile to each of the children's faces. They even made arrangements for Santa (Roger), to deliver the brightly wrapped gifts. Though Roger was reluctant to don the outfit, once he arrived at the home of those children and saw their excitement, he was certain that he was in the right place, at the right time, doing the right thing.

One episode placed the middle-aged women completely out of character. They had learned of a woman whose husband had left her. The woman was in search of a better paying job but was not having much success. She had no children but was still struggling with various bills. That month, they collected the money from the *blessing box* and counted it. It came to $114.00. They decided to round it up to $125 and give her the cash. The wheels began to turn and the excitement swelled. They agreed on a certain night to tape it to her door and *ring and run*. The event was duly labeled, *Operation Stealth*.

They located her house, coerced Donna's husband Paul, to drive the van, and arrived in black clothing shortly after dark. A couple of doors away, the van came to a stop just beyond the reach of the streetlight. The four women climbed out and immediately headed for the bushes on the side of the driveway. When they broke from the bushes, Gena stepped on Veronica's foot causing her to fall with Gena landing on top of her. Donna and Marcie didn't know they had fallen and were by this time, hiding behind a massive oak tree in the back yard. When they looked back, they could barely see the form of the two stragglers. Gena and Veronica were sitting behind the bushes, out of sight of the house but not out of the hearing of anybody within twenty yards. Marcie and Donna stifled their own laughs and waited for the two to join them.

They could see through the back window and noted that

the television was on. The outline of the woman was easily seen and they could tell that she was seated with her back to them. Perfect! Donna pointed out another set of bushes at the far sided of the back of the house and suggested that one of them would tape the envelope to the door while the other three hid there. Marcie was chosen because she was the smallest and fastest. Then when she was signaled, she would ring the bell and meet the others behind the bushes. The bushes were about fifteen yards from the back door and from there they knew they had a clear view and could enjoy the women's discovery. The signal was supposed to be a whistle, but they quickly learned that the only one of the four that could whistle was Marcie so they had to go with the meow of a cat. It was decided that Veronica could do the best meow so she was chosen to give the signal.

On three, the ladies made their way from the bushes. Marcie was at the back door watching her friends run for cover and thinking that this looked more like a situation comedy than a ministry opportunity. The envelope in her hand simply said *God cares*. She taped it to the glass door and awaited their signal. Donna's eyes were locked on the back door. "Now!" she whispered. No sound came. She leaned closer to Veronica and whispered louder "Go ahead!" Still nothing. Both women looked down to find Veronica flat on her back shaking her head while holding her hand over her mouth to muffle her laughter. Donna rolled her eyes, stood up, and simply shouted to Marcie, "Now!" Marcie hit the bell and scrambled to the bushes finding Veronica still on her back and still convulsed in laughter.

In short order, the back light came on and the woman opened the door. She looked around the yard then reached around to pull the envelope from the door. She opened it and saw a thick stack of five-dollar bills. "Praise Jesus! Praise Jesus! Thank you Lord!" was all she could say. Mission accomplished. After they determined that it was safe, the four comrades made their way around the house and up the street where they found Paul and the van.

To say that this episode as well as so many others gave them something to think about was beyond an understatement. Every once in a while they would mention how much fun the "E" assignments were, but they always came back to the night they successfully completed *Operation Stealth.*

MONDAY, APRIL 21

It had been seven weeks since Matt shared the test results with Tom. They were very full weeks and Tom was learning to savor every moment. Matt had told him that should he do nothing to treat his illness, he might have only six weeks to live, and Tom now silently considered himself on *borrowed time.* So Tom's day now included a routine, and as Marcie put it, *mandatory* nap. If he anticipated being up later in the evening, he added a late afternoon nap. Though he couldn't readily feel it slipping away, he knew that his energy was waning. Climbing the stairs came with more effort, and if he had a busy day with people and other details, he could feel the effects in the early afternoon. Tom didn't need to go to the doctor or have any tests run to tell that the disease was beginning to have its say in his life.

A nurse had drawn blood from Tom's arm and set him up for an infusion. Every week, Tom was scheduled to come in and have blood samples sent off to be evaluated. Each time he came, he would get a report from the previous sample and an infusion of blood and antibiotics. His infusions usually took about four hours giving him time to rest and visit with Marcie. Marcie accompanied Tom for each of his infusions and visits with Matt. Now Tom and Marcie sat in Matt's office waiting for him to enter. There wasn't much to say, so both sat there in a more reflective mood. Finally, Marcie broke the silence. "I've always liked Matt and Anne. They're just good people."

"I know." Tom added. "It's good to have a friend like Matt in the medical field. I know that he's doing everything he can."

Matt was a competent doctor and well trusted by his patients. Beyond his medical knowledge, he had a way of conveying his care to everyone he treated. He was genuine and easy going. You could see in his eyes that he cared. You could hear in his voice that he was sincere. The children were not afraid of him, and the adults knew that he would do his best to care for them. On many occasions, Matt would assess that a patient needed a financial break, and he would simply disregard the charges for his services. Not once did he share that with anyone, including Anne, but when people do things like that, word tends to get around. Matt called Tom a couple of times each week and more than once, Tom mentioned to Marcie that Matt could write the book on bedside manners. Matt had always been like that.

In college, he was the guy that all the girls wanted to date, and all the guys wanted their sister to date. His easygoing personality and caring nature attracted friends and patients alike. The rigors of medical school hadn't dampened his overt caring and concern. In the past ten years, Matt had made it a habit of going on medical missions trips. He would pack boxes full of medication that he either purchased or had a company donate. Then he would contact anyone who wanted to come and assist him and he, along with a team of doctors, would head off for a week to help wherever they were sent.

He'd been to the inner cities of South America, the jungles of Ecuador, and the shantytowns of South Africa. He hiked the mountains of Peru, China, and Viet Nam. He went anywhere and everywhere and did whatever was needed with whoever would join him. Each trip was unique and afforded Matt with enough stories to fill two lifetimes. He always arrived home with a mixture of exhaustion and elation hinting that he would never go again but knowing that in a short period of time he would be incubating plans for the next trip.

Matt entered the office and the three immediately embraced. He laid a folder on the desk and sat in the chair opposite them. "I'm afraid that other than slowing things down somewhat, the disease is still marching on. We just can't stop it." Tom and Marcie looked at their doctor friend in a way that told him they did not hold him in blame. They each knew the report would bear out what Tom had been feeling. Their hope now was that somehow through the samples and the research, they could be of help to someone else. They were not going to give up. But neither were they going to demand a miracle, though they would keep asking for one and accept it if it came their way.

Matt pulled out a bound notebook and slid it across the desk to Tom. It had Tom's name printed at the top. He patted the book and said, "Tom, it's very important that you keep a log of everything you're going through. We've got to know how the medication is affecting you. You need to write down changes in your eating and sleeping patterns, any dizziness, pain you might be experiencing, anything that's unusual." *Like death?* Tom thought. "Write down anything that would indicate changes due to the infusions." Tom agreed, and he and Marcie exited the office in silence.

WEDNESDAY, APRIL 23

Tom and Marcie found themselves in the most awkward of positions. They were attending a funeral. The husband of Jill, one of Marcie's co-workers passed away suddenly. By all outward appearances, he was strong and healthy. He was young, never smoked, and exercised quite regularly. So when the words *sudden heart attack* were used in connection with his name, most found it hard to believe. Tom and Marcie arrived early enough to find a seat about midway from the front. The crowd filed in, filling the medium sized church, and the service began. Marcie was uneasy but tried her hardest not to show it. Tom was equally uneasy and mentioned it to Marcie three times. It all seemed so strange. The thought of a man dying at such a young age, coupled with the knowledge that both Tom and Marcie knew they would soon be in the same situation, gave them a strange feeling that defied words.

Walking back to the car, Tom said, "Well that was as uncomfortable a situation as I've ever been in. It's way too close to home." Marcie was silent, but Tom knew she was affected deeply by the entire episode. He had looked over at her several times during the funeral and saw how hard she fought to keep the tears from flowing. He knew that she was trying to be strong for him, and he was strangely angry with himself for having to put his bride through it. He put his arm around her as they neared the car and walked her to the passenger side. He unlocked the door and helped her in.

As she turned to get her seatbelt, he leaned toward her and said, "I know it's not going to be easy. I wish I could tell you something else." At first she didn't respond. He closed her door and walked around to his side.

When he got in, Marcie looked over at the man she had grown to love immeasurably over the last sixteen years and said, "I know you're not trying to make this whole thing hard. Believe me, I'm not blaming you for any of this." She nodded her head toward the church, and continued, "It's just that going in there and seeing Jill's husband and watching her go through all of this brings everything we're going to go through too much to life. I want to be strong. I really do. But I have so many doubts. Tom, I'm really scared!"

At this point, her tears would not be stopped. Tom held his wife and fought his own battle with tears. As he cradled her against his chest, she sobbed and held onto his arms. He held her for several minutes knowing she needed time to process all that they had just witnessed. He wished for the words that would make everything all right. He wished he could say or do something to take away the pain she was feeling. He knew all these wishes were impossible so he just continued to embrace her as they rested silently in each other's arms.

They stopped for coffee on the way home. The little café was abnormally empty, and they welcomed the solitude it gave them. Marcie's eyes were still red, so she had little interest in meeting anyone she knew. They ordered their mugs and found a place near the back to hunker down and relax. Their conversation bounced from one topic to the next and several minutes later they found themselves smiling at comments each made to the other. They never brought themselves to the point of laughter, but they exited the café stronger for the interlude. A sweet cup of coffee and quiet conversation with a loved one can bring therapeutic results.

That night, the entire family grabbed blankets and made their way to the back deck. By chance, Tom had heard on the radio there would be a full lunar eclipse that night. None of the children had ever seen one before, and after Tom gave a brief description of how it happened, the enthusiasm grew.

That's the way Tom had always been. Whenever he came across something he thought might excite the kids, he made plans to expose them to it. On a number of occasions, when they were younger, he'd stop the car to pick up a turtle crossing the road. He'd bring it home, talk to them about how to know if it was a boy or a girl, they would name it, and the next day, they would trample out to the woods or pond and let it go. He once scouted a large snapping turtle making its way across the yard toward a distant pond. He cornered it and rustled up his available kids as well as several from the neighborhood. They all jumped when it snapped a small stick in half and wisely backed up when it raised itself up in defense. Grabbing it by the back of the shell, he carried it to their master bath and placed it in the shower. Marcie raced home, with only a short amount of time to get ready for a meeting. The family scattered knowing that it would be impossible to conceal a grin when mom entered the house. They didn't have to witness her finding it. They heard it. First she gave out a high-pitched general scream. This was followed closely by one angry word—"Tom!"

Sometimes it was a full rainbow, sometimes it was a deer by the side of the road, and sometimes it was even a meteor shower. Whatever the occasion, Tom rounded up the family so they could all view whatever nature put on display. As a family, they had crawled through caves, rafted through class four rapids, rode a hot air balloon, and swam with the dolphins. Both Tom and Marcie saw the value of exposing their children to the world around them. Their wide-eyed wonder was proof that building memories was better than building monuments.

Both Tom and Marcie were sensitive to spread their time evenly among the children. They knew very well the problems that favoritism caused in a family. Tom had no siblings, but Marcie had a sister and a brother, though presently only her brother was left. She watched her parents display balance regarding discipline as well as attention. And when it came to their own children, they wanted to make sure each one got the message that they were special in their own way.

Tom and Marcie had spent much time talking about the entire dating issue. They had friends who never addressed the matter but seemed to allow their children to dictate when they were ready to date. Some of these young people faced dating scenarios as young as age eleven.

The Redden parents had decided on some things long before their oldest arrived at the age where she would even begin thinking about boys. They determined that the age of a child is a poor indicator of readiness. Dating had little to do with chronology and everything to do with maturity. They felt there were two signs of a boy or girl's maturity regarding the area of courtship and dating. Number one, they had to exemplify the ability to say no to their passions regardless of the gratification offered. They knew failure could always be found in exchanging what one ultimately wants, for what one immediately desires. Number two, the child had to be able to master the art of ending a relationship while at the same time leaving the other person's self-esteem intact.

It was communicated to Madison over and over again the type of boy she should look for as well as expectations Tom and Marcie had of the boy. He was expected to come into the house and meet them before taking her out. He was expected to treat her with utmost respect and to be responsible. That's just the way it was, and Madison had a clear understanding of the parameters they expected her to abide within.

So it was not strange for Tom to take Madison out on dates. He wanted to let her see how a man was supposed to treat a young lady. When the time came for Madison to spend time with a boy, she would be able to judge whether or not the young man was treating her with respect and care.

They went out to dinner. They went to the movies. They had picnic dates, concert dates, and hiking dates. No matter where they went, when Tom labeled it a date, the outing took on a whole new meaning and instantly became special in the heart of his young girl.

For the family viewing of the lunar eclipse, each bundled up, found a spot, and began staring at the velvet sky. The moon was just coming into view over the garage, and Matty got the first glimpse of it. "There it is!" he shouted. "That's the edge of the moon." The eerie looking orb climbed higher and higher until the entire moon was clear of the obstructing garage. The family each commented on how strange and beautiful it looked, and they followed the path of the moon until it stood straight over their heads. By this time, the night air had cooled down and the family decided that it was time to go in. Tom never made a move to gather up his blanket. Marcie spoke to him, but he never answered. With his family around him and bathed by the crisp cool air, he had fallen completely asleep.

The Reddens had always been an affectionate family. They were close emotionally, and it was easily and often expressed in a physical sense. There were plenty of hugs and kisses even as the children got older. Marcie and Tom never shied away from showing affection to each other, even in front of their boys. When the boys had friends over, Tom always gave Marcie a hug, and she was quick to reciprocate with a peck on the lips or cheek. This embarrassed the young ones, but it never seemed to dissuade the parents from conveying their love.

When the children got older, Tom and Marcie guarded the affection they showed them in front of their childrens' friends. They didn't want to publicly embarrass them. They both recalled the horrors of junior high and the ridicule that was spawned by a parent that showed too much affection to their child in front of pre-adolescent friends. So their displays of affection were relegated to a pat on the back or a shoulder hug. Tom understood there was a growing reluctance of young boys to show physical affection to their dad. Yet, he also knew that physical contact was necessary for children to feel loved and accepted. A hug could do for the soul what a sandwich could do for the stomach. So he made the adjustment. Instead of kissing his boys good-bye in front of his friends, he gave them a close fisted thump on the shoulder and told them, "go do the job!" or "get after it!" They had each grown too big for Tom to pick up and cradle in his arms, so they reverted to wrestling and tackling and bouncing off each other. Tom knew this met their need for physical contact from their father, while at the same time, it sheltered them from the embarrassment of overt affection.

Madison, on the other hand, loved the attention and affection she received from her father. He would often sweep her up in his arms and spin her around the room in a silent dance move. They would often walk hand in hand or arm in arm without hesitation. Tom's arm around her shoulder never failed to convey the love he had for his sweet daughter. Madison not only welcomed hugs and kisses in public, she expected them.

Strangely, with all that was going on medically, the family understood without ever discussing it, the importance of outward displays of affection. Even the boys would instigate a hug and a kiss from both Tom and Marcie. Mom and Dad embraced and communicated their love for each other a good bit more often. Somehow, each member of the family had reached the same conclusion that it's never wrong to say, *I love you.*

Marcie entered the living room with a directive for Tom. "Don't make plans for Friday night. Dress nicely and be ready by 5:30. We're going out."

Tom had just awoken from a nap and wasn't quite sure of his surroundings. "What's up?" was all he could manage.

"Just don't make any plans. I've got everything under control."

It wasn't unusual for Marcie to arrange their social life. She was good at it and always seemed to be planning something. Nearly always, Tom just went with the flow. He had fond memories of some of their dates. Most of the time they were simple yet fun outings. They had long walks in the woods, trips to the ice cream parlor, a movie here, and a dinner there. But sometimes their dates were a little more extravagant. Sometimes they involved a lot more detail.

One time in particular, Tom came home to a picture on the mirror in his bedroom. He could tell the digital photo was of the steps of the town hall. On the back of the picture it simply said, *Be here by 6:00.* When he got to town hall a young man approached him. He looked to be about eighteen with red hair and new running shoes. He said nothing. He just extended his hand holding an envelope. On the envelope, in large red letters was the word, "Tom." Inside was a photo of Tom's desk. Like the photo at home, directions were given on the back, "Be here by 6:20." Tom had a clear sense of what was going on. He drove to five other places collecting directions to the next venue.

Sometimes a treat was included such as a small piece of chocolate or a soda. When he had finished traversing all over town, he found himself in a fine restaurant, seated at a large table next to his wife and joined by four other couples. Each of the ladies had sent their husbands on similar excursions and each delighted in having pulled one over on their mates. The evening was filled with great food, fine company, and loud outbursts of laughter.

THURSDAY, APRIL 24

Marcie lay alone in bed, much later than she usually did. She was a morning person. She wasn't like Tom, but still, she could easily be labeled an early riser. Not this morning. She lay on her back staring at the ceiling, which in a strange and mocking way, seemed to be staring back.

How had life come to this? Things were going so well for the Redden family. She adored her husband and had no doubts about his love for her. Now she faced the very real possibility, everything they were, and everything they had, would be changed forever. She clutched the sheets at her side and choked back the tears. She was trying to be brave as if that would change the outcome of their lives.

How could this be happening? The efforts to hold her tears proved fruitless. She felt a steady flow move from the corners of her eyes and slide down the side of her head. She grabbed Tom's pillow and held it close to her chest.

Why would God allow this to happen? Can't He stop it? Can't He heal Tom? Marcie tried not to think about it but that was a waste of time. What else could she think about? She pulled a tissue from the box, wiped her tears and blew her nose.

She lay on her side curled around the pillow burying her face in the softness. Then the sobs came. She pressed her face in the pillow and screamed the way she had wanted, for so long.

FRIDAY, APRIL 25

As directed, when Friday night arrived, Tom was dressed nicely and had no plans. He wore a dark suit with thin blue pin stripes. His shirt matched the stripe in his suit and his shoes glistened with a coat of well-rubbed polish. Marcie looked fabulous! She wore a beautiful evening gown with matching shoes. It had a modest neckline that was accompanied by a triple set of interlaced pearls that her grandmother had given her. The pearls in her earrings matched those around her neck. Her hair was up with only a few strands on each side falling down about her shoulders. Tom was seated on the couch when she made her entrance into the living room. She positioned herself directly in front of him and turned a complete circle.

He greeted her with a whistle and the word, "Wow!"

"You like?" she said nodding toward him.

"What's there not to like? You look terrific! Where are we going?"

She smiled the smile of a woman who knew what she was doing and said, "That information is on a need to know basis, and you don't need to know. I'm driving."

An hour later, Marcie pulled over instructing Tom to put on a blindfold. Tom never let on, but he had a hint about where they were headed. He learned a long time ago, a major part of his *job* as a husband was to go along with his bride and let her have her fun. Fifteen minutes later, the blindfold came off and they pulled into the front entrance of "The Dennonberg Manor." It was exactly as they had remembered it. It was a two hundred year old mansion that had been converted into a restaurant. A long, softly lit driveway circled a cascading fountain and led to the front of the estate. The entire face of the building was covered with ivy and large pots were filled to overflowing with fresh flowers on either side of the main door. Behind the restaurant was a beautiful reflecting pool that was home to a dozen or so swans. Benches were spaced around the pond to accommodate *before* or *after* dinner guests. This place held special memories for Tom and Marcie. It was the place where Tom asked Marcie to marry him. They had been there only one other time in their sixteen years of marriage. It was on their tenth anniversary and it was Tom who made those special arrangements. They exited the car, entrusting the keys to the valet.

They gave their name to the matre'd and were immediately escorted to their table. They were seated near the window toward the rear of the main room. And what a room it was! A large chandelier hung in the center of the ceiling with a dozen other smaller ones filling the room with a soft glow. The table donned a white lace tablecloth with a red one underneath. The candles were tall and white and held by an ornate silver base. In the center of the table was a large bowl holding two multicolored fish with daisies covering the surface. In one corner of the room a stringed quartet played softly. The other side of the room boasted an over-sized fireplace housed by a hand carved walnut mantel.

As they sat down, they both noticed the swans in the back

pond and stared at their beauty. "This is incredible!" Tom finally said. "It's just like I remember it six years ago." Marcie smiled at Tom. It was a special smile that always drew him to her. He remembered when he first saw that smile. On one of their earlier dates, Tom had taken her to a dinner theatre. The evening was magical. When they strolled to the car, Marcie slid her arm in Tom's drawing herself to his side. He felt like a giant. As they parted that night he kissed her for the first time. She returned his affection wrapping her arms around his neck and wishing the night would never end. He softly kissed her a few more times and then began to leave. When he stepped away from her, he saw it. He saw that smile. It was a full smile. It was a special smile. It was the smile of a young woman who lived in a world that was good, and safe, and pure. It was a smile that told Tom that he was special. No matter what happened, Tom knew he could handle it as long as he could see that smile.

At the Donnenberg, the waiter came and approached their table, handed them each a menu, covered the house specials and prepared to take their drink order. Tom was just about to say something when Marcie interrupted. "We need to wait a few minutes. We have another couple who will be joining us tonight." "Very well." Said the waiter. "Please feel free to take your time." Deliberately ignoring the gaze she anticipated from Tom, Marcie looked down at her menu.

"Sooooo, how many other surprises do you have planned for tonight?" Tom said, not attempting to hide his excitement but knowing that his question was spent in vain.

"This is the last one" Marcie informed him. "But believe me, it's a good one!"

Tom stroked the back of Marcie's hand, leaned forward and said, "Just in case I forget to tell you, I think you're terrific!"

Marcie leaned forward, taking Tom's other hand in hers

and said, "Well, just in case I forget to tell you, you're right, I am terrific."

Tom just slowly shook his head, smiled, and asked, "Any chance you're gonna tell me who else is coming?"

Marcie giggled, "Not a chance!"

A few moments later, their attention was drawn to the commotion coming from the lobby of the restaurant. Those seated closest to the entrance of the dining area began to crane their necks to see who had come in. More and more heads turned as guests strained to see who had entered. The Redden's curiosity was abated when the matre'd escorted the special couple to their table. Tom came to his feet immediately and shook the hand of a man he had long admired. That night, dining with Tom and Marcie were Dr. Billy Graham and his wife Ruth.

Most of the evening was a blur, with Tom concentrating hard not to ask dumb questions and trying to sound articulate. Part of the time he spent wondering how Marcie had pulled this one off. There was no question Tom understood he was in the presence of greatness. In Tom's mind, there was equally no question he had married the greatest woman in history.

The evening ended with Dr. Graham handing Tom an autographed picture and offering a prayer for him. Not long after they had gotten in the car Tom said, "all right, are you gonna tell me how you managed that one or not?" Even as he said it, the answer came to him. Somehow Tom recalled how Marcie had once made a passing comment to him about going to high school with Dr. and Mrs. Graham's daughter. Before Marcie could tease him any further with her little quips and innuendos Tom broke in, "I know! Dr. and Mrs. Graham's daughter was in your class in high school. That's it isn't it?"

"Yep!" was all Marcie could say while laughing.

Tom's condition continued to deteriorate. He was now

sleeping about twelve hours each night coupled with two naps he now required during the day. It was now eleven weeks since he first got the news. His test results never changed though he continued with his medications and infusions. Marcie kept things quiet around the house, and the kids would often visit their father in the bedroom before they went off to school, and he dozed off again.

MONDAY, APRIL 28

Though it was still in the idea stage, Tom never let go of his plans to write something for his children to always have with them. He wanted it to be instructional and helpful. He wanted it to be something they could refer to in difficult times. He wanted it to be something that would provide for them the wisdom they needed when he was no longer able to be there. His hope was that he would produce something for his children that would cause them to read it a number of times as they moved through the various stages of life. After he was gone, his plan was for Marcie to pass the completed manuscript on to the children when she felt the time was right. Over the last several weeks, he had jotted down numerous ideas to be included in the project. He was thankful that, even though he noticed a sharp and progressive drop in his physical energy, his mental capacities had not been drained by the disease to any noticeable degree. If anything, his mental capabilities seemed somewhat sharper. He was sure this was due to the urgency of the day and his excitement to share his wisdom and experience with his beloved children.

Tom was wired to have a plan. The fact that he was even writing to his children bore witness that he was most comfortable when he had a plan. Tom enjoyed routine and felt a sense of safety when he had a direction to go in. So late one morning, Tom shuffled to his study still wearing his robe. He positioned himself at his desk to begin the task of writing. He had completed a rough outline and established the direction he wanted to go. Sitting in front of him now were the ten key points he wanted his children to grasp. He had so much more to say, but he forced himself to narrow the field to the top ten things he was sure they would need. He felt confident that if they could but hold onto these guidelines at least somewhat tightly, they would be all right, no matter what life threw at them. He was thankful for all the classes he hated in high school that now enabled his fingers to fly across the keyboard. Finally a title came to his mind. It was something that would fit his life circumstances, as well as grab the attention of his young children. As he stared at the monitor, he found himself banging away at the keys. In bold print, centered at the top of the page, were these words, *That's All I Have To Say.*

He began his communication to his young loved ones with a letter from his heart. It served as an introduction to the lessons they would be receiving from him. Several times he had to pause to gather himself as he pictured his children reading his words for the first time. He labored over the opening but finally completed it. It read:

To my sweet, sweet, children,

The fact that you are reading this letter means that I have already gone on ahead of you. Please understand, this is not what I wanted or planned. I wanted to be there for you, and with you, as you grew into the great people I know you will become. Although I cannot be present with you, my hope is that the words on the following pages will speak to your hearts and minds and equip you to be successful in everything you do and everywhere you go.

Until I see you again, please pay close attention to the ideas I am sharing with you. I know they will put you in a position to enjoy your lives and help you avoid many of the pitfalls that are simply a part of life.

Please know that I love you, and I await our reunion.

All my love,

Dad

Now the job was at hand to begin writing all he knew regarding the ten principles staring back at him from his legal pad. Tom stretched widely, rotated his neck, and took a deep breath. He placed his hands on the home position on the keyboard and began to transfer his knowledge from his head to the page.

#1-ALWAYS HAVE A PLAN

"You know, I've always been a planner. I have saved myself countless hours and problems simply by slowing down and coming up with a good plan to go by. The plans I've made have allowed me to get so much more done than if I had just gone about things in a haphazard manner. I've always been that way. But most people don't have any type of plan for their lives. They plan their day, and they may plan an outing. They may even plan for retirement. But by and large, they don't have any real plans for their life. Because of this, they miss a lot of the exciting experiences life has to offer. I'm not saying that you have to plan every last detail of your life. There is room for spontaneity. But I know this, 'Where there is no plan for the future, there is no power in the present.'

When I was growing up, we had a neighbor named Mr. Martin. Mr. Martin was an old man who had been blind for many years. He and his wife were always kind to me, and I remember my Mom and Dad would often go over and visit them on summer evenings after dinner. Whenever my father would suggest we all go over their house I would always get so excited. It seemed like Mrs. Martin always had some fresh lemonade and warm cookies. The Martins and my parents would visit for about an hour or so, and I would just sit on the front steps, sip my lemonade, munch on my cookie, and listen to the conversation of grown ups. Mr. Martin had been a sergeant in WW II and stormed the beach at Normandy. After the war, he came home and made a living selling cars and investing in various businesses. Among other things, he had traveled around the world, been a professional boxer, hunted big game in Africa, met the President of the United States, and worked as a powder monkey in a rock quarry. He could tell the greatest of stories, and my family would talk about them for the next several days.

One night, I found myself perched in my usual spot with my back against the post on their front porch. I was finishing up my third cookie, making sure that I nursed my lemonade so I would have something left to wash it down with. Mr. Martin had just finished a story about driving a cab in New York City. Then he leaned forward in my direction and said words that I'll never forget. He said,

'Tom, do you know why most people are unhappy?'

I didn't even bother to answer. I just slowly moved my head from side to side as if he would notice.

'Most people are unhappy because they don't have any sense of accomplishment. They don't feel like they've done anything worthwhile. And do you know why most people feel like they haven't done anything worthwhile?'

Again, I gave the same sign of ignorance.

'Most people don't feel like they've done anything worthwhile because they haven't. But do you know why they haven't?'

So far, my sign had been working well, so I gave it yet again.

'Most people haven't done anything worthwhile because they simply haven't planned to do anything worthwhile.'

I didn't answer him. I just nodded and looked down into my empty glass. He leaned even farther toward me and said,

'Listen! Where there is no destination, there is no direction. Where there is no direction, there is no plan. Where there is no plan, there is no progress. And where there is no progress, there is no power.'

He ran his hand across the gray hairs of his head and added,

'Tom, if you'll remember that, you'll save yourself a lot of trouble, and you'll see some great things happen in your life.'

Then he sat back and smiled.

'And someday, when you're two hundred years old like I am, you'll be sitting on your front porch telling stories to a little boy who lives down the street.'"

Tom reflected on so many people he'd met who never had a plan. They never thought things through and they always seemed to have self-induced problems. He remembered Mr. Barton, who lived next door to Tom's boyhood home. Mr. Barton was a fun loving energetic man, who seemed to attack everything he did with reckless abandon. It seemed he was forever getting himself into trouble because he didn't think things through.

He once bought a television off the back of a delivery truck. It was a great deal and he couldn't turn it down. He was elated at his purchase until he found it didn't work. The amount that it would cost to fix it was almost what he would pay for a new one.

Tom never said anything but often wondered if this malady

ran in Mr. Barton's family. One time Mr. Barton and his brother *planned* a hunting outing to Canada. They bought their licenses through the mail and arrived safely getting ready to bag the largest of deer. The trip was cut short when they discovered the season ended the day before they arrived. Fortunately for them they happened to run into a game warden who shared with them the bad news.

Tom remembered Mr. Barton sharing with Tom's dad how he planned to build a boat. He had bought some plans (which was surprising because he rarely planned anything) and immediately set out to modify them (which was not surprising, since his entire life seemed to be a modification of some sort.) For weeks, Mr. Barton slaved away in his basement. Those on the outside could hear him toiling away on the inside with his saw, sander, and drill. Finally, the day came when the dingy was ready to be checked for sea-worthiness. The local lake was chosen for the task. Mr. Barton asked Tom's father and another neighbor, Max, to assist in getting the small craft out of the basement. Tom went along possessing all the natural curiosity of a small boy.

In the basement of the house was the object of Mr. Barton's time and effort. Tools were laid here and there, and the floor seemed to be completely covered in sawdust. He even noticed saw dust clinging to the spider webs that hung from each corner of the room. Tom remembered the familiar smell of varnish and paint—a smell he considered in his adult years to be like perfume to his senses. His father was fairly talented with his hands and enjoyed various woodworking projects of his own. So he had to resist examining Mr. Barton's project with an overly critical eye. Tom always felt that he had inherited his love and appreciation for woodworking from his dad and often thought of him while in the middle of a project.

Both Tom and his father were slightly surprised to find the small boat didn't look half bad. As he ran his hands over the various parts of the vessel Mr. Redden complemented his neighbor on the fine job he had done. A fresh coat of brightly colored paint gave the boat a professional look and brought a broad smile to the face of the crafter. The question in each of the men's minds was whether or not the project would be waterproof. Tom remembered Max commenting, "She sure is beautiful! But a pretty boat on the bottom of the lake is still a pretty boat at the bottom of the lake." Mr. Barton didn't seem to take offense at the comment and everyone knew the purpose of a boat was to do more than just look pretty.

The men set to getting the boat to the truck that would carry it to the lake. In short order, they realized that Max's comment about the ability of the boat to float was the wrong one. The question they should have been asking was, *How do we get this thing out of the house?* They quickly discovered that Mr. Barton had built a boat that would neither clear the doorway nor make it around the corner of the hall. They measured and re-measured. They came up with idea after idea. But try as they might, there was no way to get the boat outside. The embarrassment of their neighbor was palatable. The two men felt so bad for Mr. Barton and felt helpless to offer a solution. As they left the house, Max made the statement, "A pretty boat in the basement is still a pretty boat in the basement." Tom remembered that his Dad nodded and smiled but didn't laugh. The last Tom remembered, Mr. Barton had disassembled the craft and had it stored in his garage. Two years later, the Bartons' moved away without the boat ever making it to the lake.

Tom continued to write. "Although I was never in the military, I somehow learned that living a disciplined life was the way to succeed. The world has it backward. The world will tell you, true freedom is found in doing whatever you want. That's only true in the short run. People run toward whatever gives them pleasure at the moment and label themselves free. The problem is they trade what the want ultimately for what they want at the moment. So many people feel that the use of alcohol and drugs and getting in bed with whomever they want is the essence of freedom. In the long run, they find the opposite is true. Ask anyone with cirrhosis of the liver, or a drug addict, or alcoholic, if they feel free. Ask anyone with herpes or AIDS if they feel free. If they are honest with you, each of them will undoubtedly say no. They wish they hadn't exercised their *freedom* with so much abandon. They don't feel free. They feel enslaved to the very thing they thought would bring them freedom.

Now ask the person who has been faithful to their mate, or the person who never drank alcohol, or never smoked a cigarette, if they feel free. Because they have chosen to live within certain boundaries, they have avoided the problems that exposure to these things brings. They feel free. True freedom does not come in doing whatever you want. True freedom is found, over a period of time, in the form of living a disciplined life.

In college, what I lacked in intellect, I made up for in discipline. I did my best to get all early morning classes. While my classmates were fighting to get into the later classes so they could sleep in, my plan was to have all my classes done before lunch. I would finish lunch, study for a few hours, have dinner, study a little more, and then have all my evenings free. When I had a class that required a major writing project, I would get all the books I needed on Friday night, and then begin the assignment on that first Saturday. Because of the way I disciplined myself and stuck to my plans, the guys I lived with nicknamed me *The Spartan.* Sometimes they put pressure on me to waver from my plans, but I never got sidetracked. I noticed that as the years went by, I never panicked like they did. I never handed an assignment in late, never pulled an *all-nighter,* and I never needed an extension. I watched them pour over their work in a rush to meet the deadline, but I was never in that position because I planned ahead.

Every year, when I was a boy, the carnival would come to

my hometown. I always went but never had enough money to ride all the rides and play all the games I wanted. The summer I turned eight, I decided to come up with a plan to make some money. I wasn't afraid to work but knew that nobody would hire me. I wanted to mow lawns like my cousin Pete did, but he was older, and I was certain my Dad would never let me. I wandered around town looking for coke bottles to return for money. I found a few and returned them, but was far from having enough to really enjoy the carnival. I thought about having a lemonade stand but knew from past experience that it was not a worthwhile venture. I sat on our front steps and dreamed of finding a buried treasure big enough to fund all my boyhood adventures. Shortly, I became bored with this and returned to seeking a way to come up with some cash.

Then it hit me! Just a block away from our home they were building a community center. They had started a few weeks earlier, and it provided hours of entertainment for my buddies and me. We loved watching the heavy equipment work. After the men went home, the entertainment continued as we played around the construction site.

These are the things that I knew: It was hot out. The men were thirsty. And nobody would come by and spend money at a lemonade stand. So I decided to bring the lemonade stand to them. I set my alarm clock for 7:30 a.m. everyday, went to the kitchen, and filled a five-gallon container with water and powdered lemonade. I mixed in some ice, grabbed a handful of paper cups, and pulled my business along in a wagon. The men loved it and bought me out everyday. At five cents a cup, the money was coming in fast. My mother wasn't too happy with me getting up and going over to the construction site, but my father calmed her fears and encouraged me to keep going. He knew I wasn't getting into trouble and was openly proud of my efforts. After doing this for a week, and cleaning out our home of lemonade, they made me buy my own powdered mix. Since the money was adding up, I had no argument to offer. I expanded to add tea to the menu and before long was making my way with a wagonload of goods. I sold lemonade, tea, doughnuts, and bags of pretzels and peanuts. I decided on peanuts and pretzels because I knew that it would make the men thirsty and increase what they would drink. Each afternoon I would make my way to Murray's grocery store and restock my supplies.

Before long, I became sort of a construction site mascot. The men nicknamed me *bags,* which was short for *moneybags* because my pockets were always full of change. I had my plan and I worked it. I never told any of my friends what I was doing because I greedily didn't want them cutting in on my business. When the carnival came to town that summer, not only was I equipped to do everything I wanted, I even paid for some of the entertainment of three of my closest friends. It was a great summer of hard work and lots of fun, all because I had found a plan that worked.

That's so important! You've got to come up with a plan for every aspect of your life. This is not to say that there aren't times for spontaneity. There's plenty of room for that. But a good plan in the major areas of your life is absolutely vital if you're going to be successful. So come up with a plan. Try the plan out. If it's a good plan, stay with the plan until you come up with a better plan. Determine what you want to do, understand why you want to do it, and then find a way to get it done.

At the end of every December, for at least the last twenty years, I have set aside some time to plan what I wanted to do in the upcoming year. I never call them resolutions. I call them goals, and I've shared them with each of you from time to time. I have categorized my goals into five different areas. I sit down and develop intellectual, physical, financial, spiritual, and adventure goals.

The intellectual goals have to do with learning. I want to

be an expert at something. I want to keep learning. So I have taken courses, attended debates and lectures, and read over thirty-two books in one year.

My physical goals have to do with taking care of my body. I want to be healthy enough to enjoy all the activities that interest me. I want to be able to enjoy hiking, climbing, swimming, and biking. So I try to watch what I eat, exercise, and rest. Because of that, I've been able to participate in lots of activities, especially the ones that we share together.

Financially, I want to be able to provide for my family and enjoy doing some of the things that it takes money to do. Remember all our vacations? They only came about because I've planned to save the money for them. Because of these financial plans we've been able to do so many things that we've wanted to do.

Spiritually, I've always tried to grow. I know that just as people develop physically and mentally, people develop spiritually. So I set out each year to stretch myself spiritually. Sometimes it comes in the form of a certain type of fasting. Sometimes it is found in maintaining church attendance or going to a conference. Because I have determined to meet various goals in this area, I've read my Bible cover to cover several times, developed a deeper prayer life, and have grown as a follower of Christ in innumerable ways.

The adventure goals I set each year are there just for fun. I pick one or two things that I want to do and then develop a plan to make them happen. I've parachuted, scuba dived, flown a small plane, went hang gliding, fished in Alaska, and traveled to various other countries. Besides providing a thrill, each of these adventures has given me wonderful stories to tell.

Each December, I would sit and analyze how I did on my goals. I don't always meet my goals but I know that I've done so much better and completed so many more things because of setting goals than I would without them.

Planning has always paid off. The better you plan, the less chance you have of making mistakes. The sooner you put a plan into action, the more time you have to correct any mistakes you make."

Pushing himself away from the keyboard, Tom remembered a neighbor named Nathan. Nathan was a physics professor at the local college. He was an amiable fellow and eventually the two grew close, spending time helping one another with various chores and projects. Nathan was interesting to talk to, and had an easy way of explaining things that Tom didn't quite understand. He explained the science of flight, the reason why geese fly in a "V" formation, and how both a bullet shot parallel to the ground and a bullet dropped straight down, would each hit the ground simultaneously. He always had the latest electronic gadget and several times installed an upgrade on Tom's computer. It wasn't uncommon for Nathan to knock on Tom's door to invite him over to peer through his microscope and get a glimpse at various planets that were coming into view. So when Tom came up with an adventure idea, it just made sense to ask Nathan to help him out.

Before the children came along, Tom developed a desire to build a two-man submarine. He had read about others who had done so and decided that he'd like to take a shot at it himself. Searching both the internet, as well as the city library, he gathered up books and articles to help him in his quest. When he asked him to lend a hand, Nathan was more than pleased to do so. Nathan's job was to calculate everything involved with going under water. They needed to know how much weight was necessary to sink the vessel as well as how long they could remain submerged. It needed to be balanced both fore and aft as well as side to side. In two weeks time, Tom had a sketch of what the sub would look like. He had detailed plans on how to design it and had located a supplier for all the needed parts. Nathan had worked out all the physics and the two were ready to begin. Marcie wasn't crazy about the whole idea but understood that her husband was happiest when he was busy and in constant pursuit of an adventure. "Just don't kill yourself; I'm too young to be a widow," was all she said. Tom thought back on that comment and the irony of their present situation.

Tom had his father's welding equipment and was eager to put it to use. So early on a Saturday morning, the two men lit the torch and began their work. A month later the hull of the craft was complete. Their next task was to check for leaks. They did this by placing a light bulb inside her belly after dark. They slowly and meticulously eyed each seal looking for light shining through. They only discovered a few suspects they marked with chalk. Next, They filled the ship completely with water. A garden hose provided what they needed and they found only a few small places in need of help. They set about filling the spots in question and finished the task somewhat comfortable with its sea worthiness. Only an actual dive would be completely convincing.

The vessel would be powered by two battery driven motors. There would be eight large batteries that would supply the necessary energy. The sub would not move quickly, but they were not interested in speed. They built an air pocket in each end with a valve to allow each chamber to flood with water and a pressurized tank to empty them. The front and both sides had a Plexiglas window and lights were added to help with visibility. The entire interior was lit by a double string of fifteen watt bulbs giving them plenty of light to maneuver around inside. They had a short periscope that allowed them to stay about ten feet below while surveying the surface. The sub was even equipped with a gauge that informed them of the oxygen/carbon dioxide ratio. At Nathan's suggestion, they made removable wheels with a shaft that would receive fins for steering. The ship was equipped with two air tanks with mounted regulators in case they had to evacuate while submerged. It seems they thought of everything. They named the beautiful vessel *Sweet Lady*.

She was painted all black with the face of a gray shark, complete with open mouth, at the front. The very back of the ship carried the name in bright yellow letters. She was an eye catcher.

Three months from the start date, the final coat of paint was applied and it was time to take it to Warren Lake for a test dive. Nathan's wife Kim and Marcie went along. The sub was attached to the back of Tom's truck and rode on the inserted wheels so there was no need for a trailer. The back roads to the lake yielded stares both from other cars as well as front porches. The stares intensified at the boat landing. Some looked on with total curiosity while others, mostly men, gazed in envy. The craft was backed in the water and tethered to the dock. The men kissed their wives good-bye with promises to be careful and entered the ship. The plan was to remain on the surface for a few hundred yards and then dive to no more than forty feet. As they cruised out to deep water, Tom felt alive. This was a dream come true. How could any man ask for more than this?

When they reached deep water, they turned on the interior lights and closed the top hatch. "Let's do this thing!" Tom called out. As planned, both men gradually flooded their chambers and the sub began to sink. They turned on the exterior lights and watched as the water began to darken. The depth gauge began to move faster and faster and they slowed their decent by measuring out the flow of air in and out of each chamber. They kept an eye on each area where the ship was welded, checking for leaks. Both to their relief and delight, the sweet lady was sound. They slipped past forty feet and were able to settle her in at fifty-two. Slowly, they leveled her off and then maintained that depth as they moved about the underworld. There was very little to see—a few fish and what looked like multiple tree stumps on the bottom below. They stayed under for twenty minutes before setting their course back to the dock. When they were still a good ways out, they surfaced triumphantly to the relief and cheers of their wives. To say that their adventure was thrilling would be the definition of an understatement. They talked all the way home like two boys whose monopoly money had magically become real.

Their next dive was in the ocean. The ladies agreed to go along, having demanded a shopping spree as payment. They traveled to Wilmington and booked a hotel just a mile or two off the shore. After a trip to the mall and a hearty meal at a nearby restaurant, they settled in for a good night's sleep. Around nine o'clock the next morning, they launched off the main coast. They had mapped out where a submerged ship was and set off to explore it. After running through all their checks on the *Sweet Lady*, they set a course in the direction of the wreck. The water was fairly calm yielding a visibility of about twelve feet. They knew the approximate depth and general location, and using the inboard compass estimated where it would be. Two sets of keen eyes and a good dose of luck brought them along side their quest. They hovered next to the sunken lady being careful not to let the current drive them into the hull. They circled the old girl wanting to see her from every angle and reveling in the moment. Before they knew it, the charts demanded that they return to shore. They both knew better than to violate any of the parameters of submersion. They had been gone a total of three hours but had a sense that it was more like three minutes.

The girls should have saved the shopping excursion for the completion of the dive. They could have asked for anything they wanted and the men would have obliged. If the first dive was candy, this dive was the candy store. It was non-stop conversation all the way home. They talked about the ship, the fish, and the clarity of the water. They rattled on about several scientific points that only drew yawns and rolling eyes from the women.

Later that summer, they completed four more dives, each as glorious as the last. They explored reefs, sunken vessels, and underwater channels overcrowded with fish. Each time they finished an adventure, they began planning the next. They were like two young men who were given season passes to their favorite sporting event. The next summer mimicked the first. The toy has not been built that gave a child more joy than the *Sweet Lady* gave these men.

Almost simultaneously, two things occurred that ended the duo's adventures. Nathan was hired by a major university two states away, and a college on the coast offered to purchase their submarine for their fledgling oceanography department. The two men walked away from the deal both with a healthy profit and with an armful of wonderful stories to tell anybody and everybody that would listen.

Tom wasn't sure how long he had been walking down memory lane. He just knew he enjoyed re-visiting those special places that gave so much meaning and excitement to his life. A quick review of what he had written brought him back to the task he had started. He began to write again.

"Madison, do you remember the time we found Smithtown cavern? It was nestled in the Ramadin hills. I remember it like it was yesterday. We started out early on a Saturday morning and hiked about five miles before lunch. During our stop for lunch, we met four groups of people coming the other way. We asked each of them if they knew where the caves were. Two of them had never heard of them, and two of them had heard something about them but didn't know where they were. We decided to press on confidently because we had something they didn't have. We had a detailed map! The map was very well done and had led us accurately up to that point. Two hours later we stood at the mouth of the one of the caves. We even took a picture of us standing there. We had a wonderful time exploring the cave and returned home in triumph. We were successful because of two things: we had an accurate map, and we followed the map. Life is like that. You've got to have a good idea of where you want to go, and then you've got to be determined to follow the map you have.

John, do you remember that Christmas we put your bike together? We did it and we did it right because we followed the directions of someone who knew what he was doing.

Matty, the summer you turned three years old, we assembled our play set out back. I never saw so many pieces. But we followed the instructions and put it all together one step at a time. It worked out well and has given each of you kids your share of enjoyment.

When I asked your mom to marry me, I planned out the entire night. Permission from her parents was already granted, so I moved on to the second part of my plan, which was convincing her that marrying me was a good decision. I brought her flowers, drove her to Dennonberg Manor and slipped the ring on her plate when she wasn't looking. Of course she was surprised and obviously she said yes.

When I determined to build a shop, I spent hours laying out how it would be built and how it would be organized. Much of that time was spent in calling venders to check prices and see where the best deals were. When I did all of my homework, and I mean all of it, I began. When the entire project was complete, I found I had exceeded my budget. This is not uncommon. The rule of thumb, when you are building is, 'it always cost more and takes longer than you planned, and it's never perfect.' All of those were true with my shop. However, when everything was added up, I discovered that I was only over budget by about $50. That's not bad! I believe anybody can live with that.

When John was just seven years old, he got into a little

scuffle with a boy two doors down. Words were exchanged. and the two boys parted ways each silently vowing not to be friends with the other ever again. But that was not good enough for John. Inside he was still very mad. As he turned to go home, he saw a good size rock by the curb. He picked it up and threw it in the direction of the other boy. The rock found its mark on the back of the boy's head. He ran home screaming and John ran home in fright. We paid for the emergency room visit that included x-rays and the administering of four stitches.

It took a little while, but when things calmed down at home and John was sent to his room, we had to have a talk about what went on. Through his tears, John told us what we already knew. 'I just wanted to scare him. I didn't think that it would hit him.' It was then I told all of you about a quick rule of thumb. 'First we think, and then we do.' I remember pounding this home to you. 'Think, then do. Think, then do. Think, then do. Never do, then think! Always think, then do!' If you always think before you act, you have a much less chance of making mistakes that you'll regret. You all seemed to get it, and it has become a family mantra that has pretty much kept each of us out of trouble. W. A. Nance said, 'Failure can be divided into those who thought and never did, and those who did and never thought.' Success in life is all about having a plan.

One summer, Madison felt that she needed a job so she could have a little extra spending money. She was only seven, so her avenues were limited. She came asking for help. I told her that if she came up with a business plan, I would help her through it. I watched her get a legal pad from my office and disappear into her room. In less than an hour, she was back with four big ideas: Lemonade stand, tollbooth on our road, washing dogs, and painting rocks and selling them as paperweights. To Madison, each of these seemed like a good plan. She had prices next to each item along with some estimated expenses. She even had a financial goal listed. I tried not to laugh, but I was really struggling. The tollbooth would have made the most money but was of course out of the question. The others would have made some money but were very limited.

I suggested she sell doughnuts. She thought that was a great idea. We called for a price, and then began our planning based on that price. We knew the downtown area would be the best place to meet lots of people and decided that since most people got paid on Friday, that would put them in the best mood to buy. We ordered our doughnuts, got out two wagons for transport, and went to bed. Early Friday morning found us on the over street walkway. I had covered some basic people skills and watched Madison put them to work. She did a great job and in less than two hours she had sold 50 dozen doughnuts. She was happier than a deer in a field of corn. When we counted out her money, she had $100 but felt like it was a million.

Two summers ago, mom and I got a sense we needed to spend less money on things, and more on memories. So we asked each of you to list three things you thought would be good for us to do as a family. The requirements of the list were: they each had to be fun, affordable, and include the entire family. We called it, 'The front nine.' So far, from that list, we've had a bon fire, gone four wheeling, hiked in the mountains, gone white water rafting, and enjoyed the circus. Each of these outings has given us piles of laughter, and years of memories."

Once again, Tom found himself drifting. He didn't mind reflecting back on these memories and smiled as he thought of them as cheap and easy vacations. This time his mind propelled him to an event that took place early last spring. He remembered how all three of the kids had arrived from school simultaneously. Along with his backpack, John had come in with the mail and laid it on the kitchen table. Marcie looked through the stack and paused when she came to a particular envelope. It was brown and faded and marked urgent. In the left hand corner was a shield with a scale across the front. It was addressed to the entire family so she called all the kids together and showed them the strange looking delivery. Tom joined them from his study and smiled as Marcie slit the top edge with a knife. Inside was a letter from a law firm:

Dear Redden family,

Our firm has come across a map that, after much research, we have determined belonged to your great, great, grandfather. He was a businessman in Atlanta who, after retiring settled in North Carolina. Everyone knew him to be a strange individual who kept mostly to himself and had no outside interests. Upon his demise, his possessions were passed on to your grandfather and then your father. The estate is now defunct, but we have come across this map in our archives. Upon your receiving of this letter, please consider all of our legal obligations to you complete.

Yours truly,
Long and Associates Law Firm.

They stared in wonder at the enclosed map. It was written on parchment paper and contained lots of shapes and lines including the expected "X marks the spot" symbol. In the bottom right corner of the map were these poetic words:

To have this map is only part,
To want the find is just a start.
Happiest they who work to get,
And do not quit, though sun has set.
They see the wealth through special eyes,
The Redden fortune, here it lies.

Before anyone else could speak, John blurted out, "It's a treasure map!"

Before he could finish the word, "Map," Matty screamed, "We're gonna be rich!!!"

The whole family was now jumping up and down and yelling and dancing.

Finally, Tom spoke above the clatter, "Listen, we don't really know if this is a treasure map or not, so let's not get too carried away."

The children would have none of that type of thinking. They shouted all the more, "We're rich!! We're rich!!" Without words, Tom and Marcie knew that there was no point in attempting to douse the flames of their enthusiasm.

Tom held the map in his hands to get a closer look. "Hey, this isn't too far from here. It's over in Adam's county. I think I know where some of these places are!"

All three young hearts were unified. "Let's go right now Dad!!" they said.

"I don't know. What do you think, Babe?"

Marcie looked at Tom and then at the three whose faces were pleading beyond words. "I don't see how we can't. These three would never get to bed tonight."

"All right," Tom said. "Let's figure out what we'll need. It'll be dark in a few hours. Everyone needs to bring a flashlight. We may have to dig so John, you get a couple of shovels and put them in the back of the truck. There are some headings we need to follow, so Matty, you get your compass. Just in case we get separated, Madison, go find the walkie-talkies." In less time than it took to list all the supplies they would need, the collection had been complete. Tom began again, "Now, can you think of anything else we might need?"

John was quick to speak up. "Yeah. We need to bring some food."

Marcie nudged him and said, "An echo from the bottomless pit!"

With that she slid over to the refrigerator and began drawing things out.

Madison had a cooler on the floor and Matty made his way to the garage for some ice out of the other freezer. John showed up with a backpack and grabbed several bags of chips and pretzels, as well as some other snacks. With map in hand, the Reddens were on their way to find the family fortune. Their first destination was Wingate Bridge.

About twenty minutes later, the family scampered from the truck and gathered around the tailgate where the map was spread out. According to the map, their first destination was to be an old oak tree, twenty paces from a large rock on the opposite side of the stream. When they looked up, they saw at least a dozen large oak trees fitting the description. The ancient trees were growing in a straight line with their tops scraping the sixty-foot mark. With the sun threatening the horizon, Tom and Marcie trailed their three kids who broke into a run for the rock each carrying a flashlight, with the older ones carrying the shovels. Matty immediately started marching off the twenty paces toward one of the trees.

Before he had gotten into double digits, Madison called after him, "Matty, how do you know which tree to go for? Besides, twenty paces to you will be different from twenty paces to someone else." She had a point. Matty who already lost count, came back to the other two who had just been joined by Mom and Dad.

Tom said, "She's right. What are you thinking Maddie?"

The twelve year old took a deep breath, "Well, since the treasure was probably buried by an adult, I think Dad should walk off twenty paces. I think we need to pick one tree, and eliminate the ones beyond it. You can walk from here at one angle, and then come back and walk at the other angle.

Anything way short or way long of those two angles we won't bother with."

"Sounds good!" John said. "Go ahead Dad!"

Tom picked out one of the trees toward his left. He walked with a comfortable stride twenty paces with the family walking next to him, counting as they went. When they arrived at the tree, each family member immediately scoured the area for a clue.

"We don't even know what we're looking for," Marcie finally said.

"Clues!" Matty offered.

"Just look for anything that looks weird," John said. After about five minutes of searching, the family unanimously decided to begin again in the next direction. Tom counted out the next twenty paces, again with the aid of the whole family. When they got to the next tree, they again didn't see anything unusual. Madison stepped away from the tree. All of a sudden, she spied something small in the crux of the tree about ten feet up.

In seconds, Matty was on Tom's shoulders and had retrieved the item. It was a small brass cylinder with a solid bottom and a screw-on lid. The top came off surprisingly easily, and Tom slowly and carefully spilled out the contents. The only item in the case was a short wrench-like device. It looked like it was made of steel and was covered with rust. It was basically flat on both sides, with smooth indentations on one edge for better handling. At the far end of the flat piece was a star shaped protrusion. This they imagined went to one of the upcoming pieces to the puzzle.

Each of the family members handled the item and Tom tossed it to John with the words, "You're in charge of this. Don't lose it." John jammed it in his pocket and the family once again turned their attention to the map. A dotted line led them in a perpendicular direction from the stream. There was a drawing that appeared to be a barn of some type. But when they looked up on the small rise, they saw no hint of any building much less a barn.

When they topped the hill, the sun was gone, leaving only a glimpse of light behind. But even with their visibility hindered, they could still see the vague outline of a wooden structure at the bottom of the hill. All flashlights were on now, and the group followed the wide but faint circles of their combined lights. The building was not more than ten feet square so it qualified more as a shed than a barn. Several of the boards were missing from the side, and the bottom of the front door lay part way open touching the ground. A few random bushes were overgrown, blocking the only window to the edifice. They figured it had been used during its younger days as some type of storage building for farming supplies. The arrow on the map pointed to the right side, so everyone headed there straight away. Rounding the corner, they found nothing. They looked over the entire wall and on the overgrown grass round about. Still, they didn't see anything. Tom referred to the map several times with thoughts that maybe they were holding it wrong. Each time he looked away with the assurance that they were at the place marked by the map.

For the fourth time that night, Matty dropped his light. When it hit the ground, one light literally went out while another figuratively came on. The sound his light made when it hit the ground, was all they needed to know they were standing on the next clue.

John pushed both Matty and Marcie out of the way while he hollered, "Move!" Tom brushed away some leaves and dirt while John lifted one edge of a large board. The earth beneath the board was damp and cool. Several bugs danced away and more than a few worms retreated to the safety of the earth. All the flashlights were trained on the ground. Still there was nothing.

"Maybe we need to dig here," Marcie said. "Maybe the next clue is under the ground." Madison picked up one of the shovels while Tom grabbed the other.

"Wait!" Matty shouted. "I don't think we have to dig."

John was still holding up the vertical board. He turned his head toward Matty and said, "Yeah? Why's that?"

Matty lifted up an index finger, pointed to the board, and said, "Look!" John leaned past the large board while the rest of the family gathered around. There they found six large brass numbers nailed to the bottom of the board. Tom brushed the mud away revealing the numbers-122957.

"This is some kind of code," Tom said. "I wonder if it's a combination of some type."

Marcie pulled a pen from her pocket and wrote the sequence down on an index card. "Where to next?" she asked. Tom already had the map out and was squatting down looking for the next stop.

Tom's finger followed the dotted line leading to their next find. All along the dotted line, was the letter *N*. Each family member wondered aloud what the letter stood for.

Madison finally shouted, "North! The *N* stands for north!"

"Yeah! The *N* stands for north!" Matty said jumping up and down. Then he pulled out his compass and held it up for the group to see. "We gotta go north!"

Marcie shrugged her shoulders and said, "Makes sense." On the map, there was an *X* inside a circle to the side of what looked like a poorly drawn house.

John gave assurances that he could read the compass and argued for the right to carry the directional finder. With the same hand that held his flashlight, John pointed north, and the group got started once again. Other than the distances given at first, there was no indication of how far they would have to walk. Judging by the difference in space on the map, they agreed that it would be about ten times as far as their first clue. Because the moon was in its crescent phase, and clouds covered it intermittently, they got little help from its glow. As they moved along, each person alternated his beam of light from the ground in front of them to the landscape up ahead. They trudged over streams, and through bramble. They climbed over rocks, and under branches. All the while, John kept adjusting their course and making sure they were still proceeding correctly.

Eventually, Marcie's light graced the side of a structure about fifty yards ahead. "That's it!" she screamed. The other lights joined hers as they made their way across a meadow. They had arrived at a very old house. To say the house had seen better days would be an understatement to the extremes. The family stood outside the front door of the building, looking at the small frame of a house that at one time must have been full of life. The yard was filled with junk. A quick glance around brought into view at least three lawn mowers, two car engines, four bicycles, a dozen tires, and one washing machine. The left side of the roof was completely caved in, the steps contained only one splintered board, and the door was non-existent.

Scanning the front of the house, the family noticed not one pane of glass was intact. More than one window had a tree growing out from it. There were two chairs on the front porch, one of which was missing a leg. Next to the chairs was a couch with almost no fabric left to its pillows. Marcie was the first to speak. "I don't think we need to be going in there." She found no resistance.

"I don't think we have to," Tom shook his head and said, "The circle is on the outside of the house." He pointed his flashlight to the side of the house and continued. "What we need to do is find some kind of a circle on that side of the house. That's where our next clue is. Listen, everybody stay close. No sense us running in every direction and tripping on all this junk."

As a group, they made their way to the right of the shack and scanned the ground looking for the circle. Much to their dismay, they found none. The side of the house only offered more junk and a big old branch that had landed on top of a stone well partially crushing its roof. Both collectively and separately their lights grazed all along the ground on the entire side of the house. Nothing. They revisited the map. They were at the correct house. They knew they were on the correct side of the house. They knew they were looking for a circle. They knew there was no circle to be found anywhere. Or was there?

"What a minute!" Madison yelled. "Let me see that map again." Tom handed the map to her, and she knelt down spreading it out on the ground.

The four remaining lights all gathered on the page. "See this circle?" she said, tracing the ring with her index finger. Maybe this is not a circle *on* the ground. Maybe it's a circle *in* the ground." She tapped the circle with her finger and then trained her light across the clearing to the well. "That's our circle!" The others agreed and the troop walked together to the broken down well. The branch that lay across the roof was forked with one part laying on the ground, and the other sitting solidly on the top. There was just enough room for one person to step between the fork and peer over the edge to the bottom of the well.

Madison quickly stepped across the branches and plunged her light into the deep darkness. Part of the stone wall was broken by the branch and Madison was careful as she leaned forward to peer to the bottom. The well was twenty to thirty feet deep and still contained a foot or two of water. "There's definitely something down there," she said with her eyes fixed on the bottom. She could faintly make out the outline of what appeared to be a bucket. It looked like the end of a rope was attached to the handle but the rest of it must lie beneath the surface of the water. The handle was sticking up but was bent over to one side. "We gotta figure out how to pull it up." Each of the family members took turns looking down into the abyss, and each agreed that there was something there worth pulling up. Only part of the spindle remained and it carried an old rope that had long since broken, leaving only a few strands hanging down. They needed to find something that could draw up the item at the bottom.

Both Matty and John volunteered to climb down, but their suggestion was quickly and decisively vetoed by Mom. They needed to find a way to hook the handle of the bucket and haul it up.

Tom quietly offered the option that they go home and wait until morning, but his idea was met by a unified "No!" that was even stronger than Marcie's objection.

John drew his light across the yard. "There's got to be something around here that we can use." His light landed on the back end of a washing machine. The machine lay on its side with the back completely exposed. John walked over to it and bent down looking in. That's when he saw something that might help. He reached in and pulled on an electric motor. The mountings for the motor were so rusty that it broke loose from its moorings with ease. "We can use the wire in the motor to make a rope and hook the bucket," he shouted while his hands went to work on the wire.

The family continued their search around the grounds to find something to aid them in their task. While Tom cleared the large branch from the well, the rest of the family wandered slowly and cautiously being careful not to move too far away. Marcie came up with an empty paint bucket and suggested they use the metal handle to make a hook. The family agreed and met again around the motor John was working on. Each time John made a trip around the motor with his hands, he pulled off about a foot of wire. In just a few short minutes, he had more than enough wire to reach the bottom of the well. Tom had already wrestled the paint can handle loose and was shaping it into a hook. John took the hook and by successive wrappings with the wire, bound the two together. All hands and eyes were now at the well.

Somehow, the entire family squeezed under the roof as John lowered the hook down to the bottom of the well. The splash of the water told them the length was sufficient. Even with all four flashlights pointed at the hook, it was still very hard to see. Every once in a while, they would get a gleam of light from the hook giving direction to John. After only a few passes, John felt the hook snag the bucket handle. No one knew how heavy the bucket was so everyone waited quietly and hoped deeply as John tugged on the wire, knowing that hopes were rising with every foot of wire that came up.

With every pull of the wire, they could hear the water exiting the bucket and John could feel the weight lesson. While the bucket was still about two feet from the top, Tom reached over and retrieved the object of their attention. He placed it on the ground, sloshing out the remains of the water. Matty reached in and pulled out a small rectangle metal object. The piece was a little bigger than a man's hand and was covered with a light film making it somewhat slippery. The box was made in a sleeve-like fashion with the inside compartment fitting into the outer casing. John picked up the item, and tried to push the inside free. Although it moved only slightly, it told him the direction the case opened. Madison picked it up and ran her hands across the entire box. On the back corner, her fingers found a small hole. If she knew anything, she knew that this was the lock to the box.

"The key!" John yelled. As he pulled from his pocket the tool he'd been protecting, and held it up for before the group. "I've got the key!"

"Let's see it," Marcie said as she grabbed the box with one hand and extended her other hand toward John. The hole was full of mud so she struggled with the star shaped metal. Tom offered her a knife and in a few moments she had it clear and had fitted the key nicely. She turned it one way and it wouldn't budge. She turned it back the other way and the inside compartment opened easily.

Inside the box was a thin piece of copper. Etched in the copper were the words, "Follow from the well, all the steps, North, East, South, and West." Madison repeated the words while all the family followed along deep in thought.

Marcie said, "Well it seems like we need to go in each of these directions."

John joined in, "Yeah, and it seems like there are only four directions we're suppose to be going. But how far and where?"

Madison asked, "What if we head each of these directions in the order they're given. Usually, you would say, 'North, South, East, and West,' But this gives those in a different order. I think we need to follow them in that order."

"What about those numbers Mom wrote down. Maybe we need to use them here," Matty entered.

Marcie pulled the paper from her pocket and held it up, "Let's see what we've got, 122957."

Tom spoke up, "If this number can be broken down into the number of steps we've got to take, then we need to travel those steps in each of the directions given." "Right!" Madison jumped in. All we have to do is see how many different groups of four numbers we can come up with. Then we need to try each of these and see where we end up."

Madison had always excelled in math and set about the task of breaking the string of numbers up into four parts. In very little time, she had come up with eight groupings. She immediately eliminated four groups because they would take them into the side of the house. A fifth one was abandoned because it took them to a large pond. Then the choices were narrowed down to three.

John gave Tom the compass, and Tom worked his way back to the well. He chose the first set of numbers calling him to go north one, east two, south 29, and west 57. With his back to the well, he began walking. The rest of the group walked with him.

He reached the third direction when Madison called out, "Wait! This isn't right! Don't the directions say *steps*? You're doing *paces*."

"That's right" Marcie chimed in. The family gathered again at the well, and this time Tom began putting one foot in front of the other and counting out individual steps. He completed the last direction and found that they were on a gigantic piece of surface rock.

"No chance of digging here," Matty said. They began again this time with the numbers, 12-2-9-57. 57 steps west put them out in the meadow. The grass pulled up surprisingly easily, and the ground beneath it appeared loose and moist. Digging would not be difficult.

Immediately, the two shovels were put to work. With the excitement of the moment bringing more and more adrenalin, they dug with speed. They each rotated the chore, and in less than ten minutes they had dug a hole four foot around and two feet deep.

Matty jumped on the end of the spade and heard a strange and hollow sound. "Hey, I found something!" he screamed. John was in the hole as fast as gravity would pull him. He was on his knees pulling at the earth and removing large handfuls of soil. Before long, he had exposed the entire top and most of each side of a medium sized wooded box. The box was brown, almost black with no distinguishing marks. It had two hinges in the back and a hasp in the front each of which was thoroughly rusted with age. There was a small handle on each side making transport of the box easier. With the end of a shovel, Tom pried the end of the box up and John finished the job by yanking on one of the handles. It was very heavy, but together John and Matty hauled the box up out of the hole where the rest of the family gathered around. This could be another clue, but somehow each of the treasure seekers knew that they had found what they were looking for.

Marcie suggested that they bring the box back to the house where Tom could work on opening it in the shop. The other four would hear nothing of the delay. With the edge of the spade, Tom was able to gain a purchase under one corner of the hasp. Then with an easy push, the screws gave way and the entire hasp came off, lock and all. When the lid was brought all the way back, the hinge screws pulled out and the lid fell to the floor of the meadow. Not a beam strayed from the contents inside.

"Yes!" John yelled as the family gazed on with all the excitement and attention of a child at a magic show. There before them lay the object of their struggle. In the blackness of the night, the flashlights moved back and forth across their treasure. The treasure chest contained a pile of gold coins, two brass urns, a picture of an old man and woman, and a small Bible.

Without hesitation, each of the children had their hands in the coins and began lifting them and watching them cascade over their wrists and back to the box.

"Can you believe this?" Marcie asked.

"I can!" Madison said.

"We're rich!" Matty yelled. Because the handles were small, it didn't make for easy carrying, but each family member took his turn in transporting the box back to the truck. An hour later, they were motoring toward home, each with an idea of how the treasure should be spent.

The box was placed on the kitchen table and the lid was removed once more. Each family member grabbed a handful of coins and began putting them in ten-dollar stacks. Ten minutes later, everything was tallied. The sum came to $300. The brass urns were not much more than decorative items. and Marcie commented on how well they would shine up for mantle display. The Bible was old and had the names of Tom's great-great grandfather and great-great grandmother. They guessed the picture bore his image and that of his wife. In short order, Madison and John realized their find made them far from wealthy but were grateful just the same.

Matty shared his feelings when he said, "Maybe you're not rich, but I am!"

Tom explained that over one hundred years ago, $300 was a tremendous amount of money. Tom and Marcie explained to the kids that if they would part with the urns and the old Bible, they felt that it would be fair to divide the money between the three children. They were met with no argument.

It was well after midnight when the Reddens found their beds. They had had a great adventure, worked well with each other, and had what the children knew was a good bit of money for their trouble. As Tom and Marcie lay in the dark, Marcie turned to Tom and asked,

"Do you think they'll catch on? Do you think they have a clue?"

Tom turned to her, "Madison might, but I doubt it. I'm pretty sure the other two have no idea. But when I watched how they worked with each other and how they figured out all the clues, and saw how excited they were, I knew it was worth all the trouble I went through last week and we got our money's worth this week." With that, he kissed his bride, and the two of them surrendered to sleep knowing they had built for their entire family a memory that would last a lifetime.

Tom looked up and saw the words on the screen looking back at him. He still had more to say. For all intents and purposes, he was gone. He was thinking on this memory so hard that he was actually reliving it, and he was unsure how long it had taken him to travel back to that memory. He slowly came back to reality with the strange realization that he was alone, and smiling. Once again, he pressed himself to the task at hand.

"Ask Mom to tell you about the envelope in her glove compartment. I knew the chances were good that Mom (and each of you) would have a car accident. Most people have an accident, and most accidents are not fatal. So I wrote your Mom a letter (she'll show it to you), and I sealed it in an envelope. The outside simply says, "Open this in case of an accident." Your Mom thought it contained directions she should follow in case of a bump up. That was in the letter, but that's not all the information I wanted her to have. What I really wanted her to know was that even though she damaged the car, I valued her and her safety much more than that. The letter in the envelope is a love letter telling her as long as she was all right, everything would be fine.

A couple of years after your Mom put that in her glove compartment, she had an accident. She rounded a corner and hit a person's fender. Naturally, she was upset and she was certain I would be mad. But when she opened the envelope and read my letter, she calmed down and took care of things the way she should.

Remember that summer we drove to New York to see my cousin Jeff? That was a great trip! I'm not sure there was any way to pack in more activity in just seven days. We toured Gettysburg, Hershey, Lost Indian Caverns, Washington, D.C., West Point, and New York City. What a trip! What a great time!"

Tom took a short mental trip to each of these places remembering the comments each of the kids made along the way. He recalled John's comment about how the soldiers probably hid behind the monuments in Gettysburg to shoot at each other. He thought about how Matty wanted to sit on Abe's lap at the Lincoln memorial. He smiled when he reflected on Madison thinking how great it would be to live in a cave. Then his mind traveled to all the other trips they had made. Together, they had been to Canada, the Grand Canyon, Florida, California, Hawaii, Bermuda, and many points in between. With a heavy sigh, Tom was thankful to be able to expose his children to so much more than either he or Marcie had experienced. He knew his kids appreciated it, and he also knew that this was part of what parenting was all about.

Tom's hands once again found the keys. He closed his first point with these words: "all of the great things in our lives happened because we had a plan and we stuck to the plan. Those who fail to plan are making plans to fail. Slow down. Think things through. Organize your thoughts and when the time is right, and not before, turn your energies toward what you want to do. When you make that a habit, you'll be able to look back on a life of fulfilling accomplishments."

Tom suddenly felt his energy drained from him. He hadn't realized how all that thinking could make him feel so tired. With the kids away and Marcie picking up groceries, the house was quiet. He made his way to the couch.

An hour later, Tom awoke feeling a good bit better and prepared to get dressed and ride into town to get the maintenance on his truck done. He was careful to take care of the vehicles in due order but never panicked when the mileage between oil changes exceeded the recommendations. After getting his truck taken care of, he stopped by to see his friend Johnny. He found him holding a belt sander and rounding off the corner of a slat to an outdoor bench he had just replaced. Johnny was a curious man. He stood well over six feet tall and weighed on the short side of one hundred and forty pounds. His nose was large but crooked, and it had been forty years since his head had carried a strand of hair. Johnny was full of energy although he was in his early eighties. He always had a chew of tobacco in his mouth and a walking stick in his hand. Never once did he fail to offer Tom a wad of chew, and never once had Tom accepted. Johnny had injured his leg in a farming accident and had since walked with a limp. The leg may have been lost except for the skillful hands of the doctors.

Johnny had been out in the field when his tractor got stuck in the mud. He worked it back and forth but could make no progress. He decided to put some scrap wood under the wheel to give him some traction. He gathered up a few short pieces and stuffed them under the wheel encumbered by the most mud. The wheel still spun because the wood was not far enough under the tire. Johnny put the tractor in gear, and while the wheel was slowly spinning wiggled the boards back and forth in order to get them further under the tire. In an instant, the wheel caught the boards and shot them through the ditch the tire had been making. In the course of doing so, it spun Johnny around and drew his leg under the moving wheel. The bones of his lower leg were crushed in pieces and blood spurted from a deep gash just below his knee. The pain was excruciating. He called for help, but no one was around to hear him. A neighbor had been passing by and saw Johnny's tractor partway through the side of one of his outbuildings. He knew there was a problem and retraced the path that led back to Johnny. The man was unconscious. The neighbor bound up the leg and called for help. Five weeks later, Johnny left the hospital convinced that the staff tried to kill him. He resolved never to return to "that torture chamber" again.

For some reason Johnny had always liked Tom. They had met at a town counsel meeting and just seemed to hit it off. They shared a love for the outdoors and an appreciation for creation. Several times each year, Johnny would fill the Redden's pantry and refrigerator with enough vegetables to last the family for months.

"What ya up to old timer?" Johnny asked trading his tobacco for a new wad.

"Rumor has it yer dyin." Johnny never was blessed with the gift of subtlety.

"That's what they tell me," Tom said matching Johnny's directness.

Johnny tapped the ground in Tom's direction with the end of his stick. "That's a shame. You're one of the good ones. It always seems to happen to the good ones. Margaret and me been prayin' for ya."

"Thanks," Tom said. "I sure can use it. How you been getting' along?"

"Pretty good for a fifty-year-old," Johnny said with a chuckle in his voice. "I can still get out of my own shadow and get into one when Margaret's huntin' me down for something," he said nodding toward the back door. He gave a wide grin revealing three crooked teeth on the bottom and a wide gape where two absent teeth had been on the top. "Lately, I think she just wants me around for my good looks." He shook his head and continued, "Did I ever tell you about the time I got contacted to be in the Adam's county handsome man contest?"

Tom shook his head, "No, I don't think you did."

"Well, I never did get contacted. I was just wonderin' if I lied to you about it!" He gave a grin bigger than the last one. Tom joined him in the grin and shook his head. Johnny continued without loosing his grin, "When God was giving out good looks, he said, 'come forth' and I came fifth."

He began laughing before he quite finished the last word, and Tom joined him as if he'd heard that one for the first time although he knew that Johnny had told him the same joke at least four times before.

But that was one of the things Tom liked about Johnny. He was the real deal. No pretensions. No false humility. What you saw was what you got. There was something attractively refreshing about that. Johnny didn't pretend to be anything other than what he was, so it gave Tom permission to be himself. What a relief!

The men continued to talk on various subjects such as honeybees, blue birds, painted turtles, and a white Herron that had made its home in Johnny's pond. Tom left with a hug from Margaret and three cans of beans. He reflected on his time with Johnny and smiled most of the way home shaking his head as he went.

TUESDAY, APRIL 29

That afternoon, Tom and Marcie landed home after a long visit to the Doctor's office and time at the clinic. More blood was drawn and Tom was given another infusion. The test results revealed that although the disease had slowed down, it was still progressing in the same direction. Because of the way Tom felt, he didn't expect any other result. Marcie, on the other hand, was visibly disappointed. Each time they went to the doctor's or clinic, she was hoping to get some news that the sickness had been stemmed and that somehow things had begun to reverse themselves. She always tried to put on a good front, but each time Tom could see right through her and answered the call in bolstering her spirits. Usually, by the time the ride home was completed, Marcie was back up to the task again and had set her sights on supporting and encouraging Tom.

THURSDAY, APRIL 30

Tom carried his coffee to the back deck, still wearing his robe and slippers. He dropped into one of the cushioned chairs just as the sun was beginning to peak through the trees. The air was fresh and clear, and he could hear the earth announcing the beginning of a new day

It promised to be a pleasant day, but a storm was raging in Tom's soul. He felt a foreign feeling of heaviness on his heart. He knew the cause but not the solution. Tom was a *fixer*. He always fixed things. It didn't matter if it was a presentation gone haywire or the toaster. He'd get out the "tools" and have it back up to speed in no time.

But this was something far beyond his abilities. There were no tools to *fix* him. He tried to pry it from his mind, but like an overplayed song, it just kept forcing its way back in— dominating his mind and pressing in on his spirit. He didn't understand. He couldn't understand.

He had so much to live for. In an age where so many people toss their lives away, Tom sought to squeeze out every ounce of living he could. He had a wonderful wife and three great kids. He had the family so many dreamed of. His job was going well, and he was making more money than he ever had. He had lots of friends and a house full of great memories. He was a good guy. He hadn't done anything to screw up his life, like so many other guys he knew.

How could this happen? The questions pounded on top of him like a torrent of water from a river. *Why this? Why now? Why me?* Before he understood what he was doing, he heard himself say, "God, what did I ever do to you to deserve this? Why is this happening?" Then with no attempt to stifle it, he looked up and screamed, "What do you want from me?"

The tears came followed by the sobs. The pain in his heart

was more than any two men could bear. He had held it together for too long. Now the dam had burst and everything inside him was spilling out. He leaned forward with his elbows on his knees and dropped his face into his hands. "God, I'll do whatever you ask me to. I'll go anywhere. I'll be anything. Just let me live! God, my family needs me. I don't want to die!"

FRIDAY, MAY 4

Traditionally, Friday night was home-made-pizza night at the Redden's. The island in the kitchen was covered with various toppings and each member was given the dough and the freedom to make whatever kind of pizza their taste buds beckoned for. Matty usually got the unofficial award for the most toppings while Madison simply had extra cheese. Every once in a while someone would bring up the time the family had a food-fight on pizza night. Surprisingly enough, it was started by Marcie who always kept her kitchen neat and in order. On this night, John tossed the large spoon into the sauce jar splattering Marcie's plate and shirt. She returned fire but got most of it on Madison who covered Marcie, John, and Matty with a mixture of sauce, cheese, and mushrooms. In an instant, the ingredients were flying all over the place. A truce was called after Tom was smeared by thousand island dressing and Madison had a cherry tomato smashed in the back of her pants. The family cleaned it all up while what was left of their pizza creations baked in the oven.

The truce was still in tact and each member of the family dutifully went about the task of eating their masterpieces. After the meal, everyone settled into a spot on the couch to watch a movie. Being that it was a Friday night, Tom and Marcie allowed the kids to sleep in the living room. They decided early in the parenting process, that they would say yes to their children's requests as often as possible. They knew they would have to say no more often than most parents because they felt strongly about the various activities available to young people. The shows they watched, the music they listened to, the clothes they wore, and the movies they viewed, were all carefully monitored by Tom and Marcie. So they developed the habit of processing every request through a *why not?* grid. If it wasn't dangerous physically, emotionally, or spiritually, and they could afford it, they usually said yes.

Among many other activities, this attitude had allowed the kids to sleep in their clothes, eat spaghetti for breakfast, watch television on the back deck, build a *slippin' slide* on the lawn, and paint their rooms to match their personal taste. This gave the Redden children a sense of freedom while at the same time built parameters by which Tom and Marcie could sleep.

Sometimes it was the parents that pushed things beyond the normal boundaries of life. One day, when Madison was in fifth grade, she had had a particularly bad day at school. Apparently she had been picked on a bit, did poorly on a quiz, and overall just felt a bit overwhelmed by life. When Tom came home, Marcie filled him in on the life issues of their oldest. Tom opened Madison's door to find her on her bed with her pillow over her face.

"You in there?" he quietly asked. Madison knew there was no need to answer.

Tom gently sat on the edge of her bed and took her hand. "Mom told me you had kind of a rough day today. You wanna talk about it?" Still no answer. Tom continued, "Did I ever tell you about Mrs. Regal, my first grade teacher?"

Tom wasn't sure, but he thought he heard a muffled, "No."

"Well, Mrs. Regal was the meanest teacher in the whole school, maybe the whole world. No one really knew why she was so mean. Somebody told me that she came from an orphanage and that everyday they made the kids drink pure lemon juice for breakfast. The story was that she was a witch and that at her house she had some shrunken heads of some of her former students." Madison's pillow gave way to her eyes. They told Tom to continue. "She used to call us names and give us double homework on the weekends and holidays. If we did anything wrong, anything at all, we'd have to stand facing the corner for the rest of the day. And she'd make us wear a hat that had donkey ears in it. Everybody hated her."

Though her mouth didn't say anything, Madison's eyes said, "Really?"

Tom went on. "Well, one day, Tommy Jennings gave me a piece of gum on the playground. We finished playing kick ball and filed back into the classroom.

I had just started my afternoon work when all of a sudden I heard, 'Thomas Redden!' I froze. My mind raced trying to think of what I had done wrong. Then it hit me. I forgot about the gum in my mouth.

'Come up here!' she yelled.

I walked up to the front of the room.

'Is that gum in your mouth?'

I was too scared to answer so I just nodded my head. She put her hand in front of my mouth and told me to spit it out. I did and headed back to my seat.

She had a hold of the back of my shirt and said, 'Not yet!'

She backed me up to the front of the entire class and put that gum on the end of my nose. The whole class started laughing. I was so embarrassed that I started crying, and that made the class laugh even more. Even Tommy Jennings was laughing, and he was my very best friend in the whole world— well, at least in the entire first grade. I sat at my desk with that gum on my nose just sobbing away.

Finally, after about five minutes she came by my desk with a trash can and let me throw it out." Tom let out a deep sigh. "Boy, as long as I live, I'll never forget that day. Do you know that every once in a long while, when I put a piece of gum in my mouth, I still think about that day, way back in first grade?"

Madison's pillow was now on the floor. She sat up and rubbed her daddy's back, "Daddy, why do some people have to be so mean?"

Tom turned to her, stroked the side of her face, and said, "I'm really not sure. I guess some people think they can make themselves feel better by making other people feel worse. But if you understand something, it can make things a whole lot easier."

Tom continued with a sense that he was at the top of his fatherhood game. "Listen. There are only four types of people you're gonna meet in your entire life." Tom held up four fingers representing each of the people he was talking about. As he talked, he touched each of the fingers with the index finger of his other hand. "You'll meet some people that will like you for the right reason. You'll meet some people that will like you for the wrong reason. You'll meet some people that will hate you for the wrong reason. And you'll meet some people that will hate you for the right reason. Now there's only one group that you really have to worry about. Which group do you think that is?

Madison's brow furrowed the way it always did when she was thinking hard. She pursed her lips and slowly moved her head from side to side indicating that she wasn't even going to guess. Tom jumped in. "The last group is the only one you need to worry about." Tom grabbed his first two fingers. "You see, if someone likes you for the right reason or the wrong reason, who cares? At least they like you. If someone hates you for the wrong reason, who cares? Their reason for not liking you is the wrong one. They are wrong, not you." He grabbed his fourth finger and bounced it between them for emphasis. "But if someone doesn't like you for the right reason, then you are wrong. You've done something wrong and they are right in not liking you for it.

Now the great thing is, the last group is the group that we have most control over, because a lot of the time, we can stop doing the things that cause those people not to like us. Does that make sense?"

Madison had a particular look on her face. It was the face she donned when something deep and important was sinking in. She nodded slowly and said yes in a way that convinced Tom the lights were on and she was making the truth her own.

Tom bounced his shoulder against his daughter's. "Hey, I've got an idea. Dinner won't be ready for about forty-five minutes. I've got to go into town for more copier paper. Why don't you come with me?" Tom stood up and Madison swung her legs off the bed indicating that she would go. A few minutes later they were in the car pointed toward town.

On the way back, Tom suddenly pulled into the empty parking lot of a local business. He parked the car in back of the building and told his confused daughter to get out.

She met him in front of the car with the obvious question, "Daddy, what are we doing here?"

Tom grabbed both of his little girl's shoulders. "You my young lady are growing up so fast. It's time you started driving."

Madison backed up. "What? I can't drive!"

"I know," Tom said. "That's why we're in the parking lot and not on the highway. Don't worry, I'll teach you."

She had been on her Father's lap before and had moved the wheel as they slowly went through their little neighborhood, but this was different. Behind the wheel she listened as Tom gave her a few minor instructions. She adjusted the seat, put her foot on the brake, placed the car in gear, and slowly rolled forward. The entire time, Tom was encouraging her and coaching her along. The parking lot was large and free of cars, and before long, Madison felt quite comfortable tooling around the lot. At one point, as if she needed an additionally adrenalin rush, Tom instructed her to pick up speed along the far side of the lot. When she reached thirty-five miles per hour, he backed her down to conclude their ride. Madison was beaming. As they traded places for the ride home, Madison gave the man in her life a firm hug.

All through dinner, Madison jabbered on about their adventure. More than a few times Tom caught Marcie's face that told him without words that he had scored major points with both his daughter and his wife.

When he kissed her goodnight, she squeezed him extra tight and said, "I can't wait to go to school tomorrow! I think you're the best Daddy in the world!"

Tom poked her little nose with his and said, "That's all I ever wanted to be."

SATURDAY, MAY 10

It was well after eleven when Tom finally stumbled out of his room. The kids had already eaten breakfast and were elsewhere while Marcie cleaned up the dishes. He greeted her with a kiss and a bear hug and then wandered over for some coffee and a glance at the paper.

A few minutes later, Marcie joined him with her cup. "Mom and Dad are coming over to spend the night and to come to church with us tomorrow. They want to take us out to dinner. How's that sound?"

"Sounds like a free meal! I'm in," Tom said without looking up. He had grown accustomed to being informed and advised rather than consulted, and for the most part had adjusted to the change rather well. He was never much for surprises, but as his life had changed of late, his attitude had too.

Marcie's parents arrived with the usual fanfare and the seven of them enjoyed a wonderful meal at Tom's favorite restaurant. The evening was filled with laughter and each member complaining of eating too much. Shortly after arriving back home, Tom headed for bed while the kids enjoyed a movie in the game room. Marcie stayed up late visiting with her Mom and Dad and for the first time, relayed to them her feelings.

As they sat on the couch her eyes welled up. "I'm so scared," she said. "I try not to think about it, but everyday, I watch Tom get a little more tired and lose a little more strength. He's got a great attitude about the whole thing, but sometimes I don't know what to do or say."

Marcie's Dad leaned forward and placed his elbows on his knees while Marcie's Mom faced her and took her hands. "Honey, I think you're doing a great job," he said. "Nobody expected this and nobody knows completely how everything is going to go. Just be true to your vows and love your husband the best way you know how. You've got a great 'home team' cheering you on." The words "home team" instantly took Marcie back to another time and another place. She remembered when her Dad had first used that phrase.

Marcie and her older brother Richard, now in the army, and stationed in Korea, had entered a season of continual fights with each other. They fought over seats in the car, desserts, the phone, and anything else deemed insignificant by everyone else. Later, it manifested itself in both of them becoming very critical of each other. It drove their parents crazy. They couldn't get through to the children how childish it was and how frustrated they were.

Finally, Marcie's Dad sat the two of them down and asked

a question. "If you each were on a sports team, would you rather play a big game at home or away?"

In a rare exhibition of agreement, both of them said, "home."

"Why?" their Dad asked thrusting both hands out.

"Because you're used to your own field," Richard offered.

"Why else?"

"Because you don't have to travel," Marcie suggested.

"Close. Why else?"

After a pause Richard gave an answer that sounded more like a question, "Because the people in the stands will be cheering for you."

"Right!" their Dad said, standing up. "When you're at home, the fans cheer for you. When you're away, everyone boos you. That's the problem you two have. You're part of the home team but you're acting like the visitors." Neither childrens' faces registered cognition. Dad continued, "You guys are supposed to cheer for each other but you spend all your time booing each other. From now on you're going to be part of each other's home team. You're going cheer for each other, support each other, and encourage each other. No more criticizing, no more, poking fun, no more fighting. You understand?"

Both children seemed to understand but were afraid to acknowledge it with more than a nod of the head. "And one more thing. If you can't act the way a fan is supposed to act, then you will be escorted from the stadium. Do either of you know what that means?" Neither of them did, but they were equally afraid to admit that. "It means that you will have to go and sit in the cheap seats. Namely your room—until you can behave the way good fans do. Any questions?" Seeing none, their Dad left the room ending with the words, "The game starts now."

Now Marcie was being called upon to be on Tom's home team—to cheer him on and encourage him. To be there to help him any way she could. She always felt that she was his biggest fan. She always believed in him and always bragged on him. But this was so much more than a game and in this scenario there was no second place.

They spent the rest of the evening talking, laughing, and crying. In bed that night, Marcie breathed a prayer of thanks for such good parents.

SUNDAY, MAY 11

Sunday brought church, lunch at a restaurant, and warm good-byes from Marcie's folks. Tom put on some sweats, located the couch in their room, and settled in for some shut-eye. Marcie napped in the living room, and the children scattered to the outdoors.

When Tom awoke, he sat up but remained still for quite awhile. He had slept hard but was having trouble shaking the cobwebs out. He took a few deep breaths and forced himself to stand up and stretch. Slowly the motivation to move crept in. He wandered through the living room pausing to wink at Marcie who was nestled on the couch under a blanket. Her one eye was partially open, and she wiggled two fingers at him. He gave a half smile and meandered toward the study. He had some ideas he wanted to put in ink.

#2-NEVER WALK AWAY FROM GOD

"Because of what's happening to me, you will face the temptation to be mad at God and walk away from Him. Don't do it! There are only two things that you will still have 100 years from now—God's word and God's love. Too often we get confused and think that God's greatest obligation to us is to make us happy. While God does enjoy our being happy, His greatest desire is that we be holy. That's where ultimate happiness is found. We must not forget that."

Tom's mind immediately went to a conversation he had with a friend at a former place of employment. His name was Sean. Sean was a nice guy. He was about 29 years old and had so much going for him. He was good looking, intelligent, and moving his way up the corporate ladder. Everyone enjoyed being around him, some a little too much.

For some time, it had been the office chatter that Sean was spending a good bit of time with Lisa. She was a pleasant woman about three years younger than Sean with an attractive smile. Lisa worked in another department, but they often were found in each other's offices for a good portion of the day. Each of them was married and had a family. Beyond those boundaries Sean made it public knowledge that he was a Christian and an active member of his church. He and Tom had been in an office devotional study together for a couple of years. This made it very awkward whenever anyone saw Sean and Lisa together.

Strangely, Tom felt compelled to talk to Sean about what was going on. Tom wasn't normally a confrontational type of guy. In fact, he resisted it whenever he could. He liked people and enjoyed being liked by them in turn. But late one Tuesday afternoon, they found themselves together in the boardroom at the conclusion of a staff meeting.

Sean was seated, and was still gathering up the remnants of a report he had shared with the department. Tom took a deep breath and asked, "Sean, may I ask you a personal question?"

Sean did his best to act nonplussed but in the pit of his stomach he knew what was about to be addressed. "Sure," he said pushing the last of the papers in a folder and sitting up straight in his chair.

"Listen" Tom said. "I usually don't mess in other people's business, but it seems like you're spending an awful lot of time with Lisa. Some folks have even seen the two of you out to dinner. What's up with that?"

"Not much," Sean offered. "We just enjoy spending time with each other. She's a great girl and so easy to talk to. Of course, she's not bad to look at either." Sean was hoping that that last comment was seen as humor so as to break the tension of the moment. Tom's face indicated that the effort was wasted.

Tom measured his next set of words carefully. "Sean," he paused long enough to evaluate his next comment. His eyes stayed locked on Sean's. "You're married."

"I know that," Sean returned, pushing himself away from the table and leaning on his elbows. "But things at home aren't going so good. Donna doesn't respond to me the way she used to, the way Lisa does. She's always angry and never stops complaining. When I talk to Lisa, it seems like she's really interested, like she really cares. It's been months since Donna's shown any interest in anything I'm doing."

Tom sat down across the conference table from his friend. "Look, I know that marriage isn't always easy. Marcie and I have had our share of struggles, but we've always worked it out. Can't you and Donna go to some counseling or something?"

"Donna's suggested that, but I've been too busy. Besides, I'm just not feeling much for Donna lately. Deep down inside, I think I may have married the wrong person."

Tom was angry at Sean's mentality. He'd seen people rationalize all sorts of behavior before, and this was no different. He did his best to remain calm. "Listen, is there any doubt in your mind that I care about you?"

"No," Sean said avoiding Tom's stare.

"Then you need to know something. You're heading for an affair, and you're about to lose your wife and kids. But that's not the worst of it. The worst part is, you are walking out of step with God and in danger of His discipline."

Sean seemed outwardly edgy. He looked down pursing his lips. "I know that you care about me, but you gotta know that I care about Lisa. The simple truth is, when I'm with Donna I'm miserable. When I'm with Lisa, I'm happy. And I know that God wants me to be happy."

With great effort, Tom controlled his emotions. "Is that what you think? Do you really believe that God's main concern is your happiness? "You've got to be kidding me!" Tom got up from his chair and leaned on the table. He wasn't invading Sean's space with his body, but he was sure doing more than that with his mind. "Look, if God had a choice between your happiness and your holiness, holiness would win every time." Tom felt like a football coach addressing his team in the locker room—down 21-0 at the half. He wanted to sit back down, but his body refused. "You know what the problem with most Christians is? They think just like you, which is just like the rest of the world. Let me give you a short cut. You can spend your whole life pursuing happiness at the expense of holiness and never find it. But—if a person will pursue holiness, happiness just seems to naturally find them."

Sean gave no reply. Neither did he show any signs any of this was getting through. Tom looked out the window of the fifth story room. In a strange and hypocritical way, he wanted to choke the life out of Sean. He was quite sure Sean had made up his mind to eventually leave Donna. He also knew, once a person makes plans in that direction, it's only a matter of time before they act on it. Still, he wanted to appeal to Sean's Christian side. "Listen, let's say you're right. Let's say God's biggest goal is to make his children happy. Isn't Donna one of

His children? Doesn't she have a *right* to be happy? You know that leaving your wife and kids will make them angry, hurt, and confused—anything but happy. Why does the happiness scenario only work for you and not for Donna and the kids?"

For the first time, Sean looked up from the table. "You done?"

"Yeah, I'm done. Look, I just want you to think about some things before you throw your life and your witness away. O.K?"

Sean gave a half smile and quietly said, "I got some work I gotta get done." With that, he made strides to the door and exited, leaving Tom to stare out the window and shake his head.

Within two months Sean had left the company as well as his wife, had moved in with Lisa, and was on the road to *happiness*. Life was so good. Just over a year later they were married, and life couldn't get any better for Sean. That is, until two years later when Lisa met another co-worker and decided he was a better catch than Sean. Three months later they were separated and heading for divorce court. Sean gave some fleeting thoughts of going back to Donna, but the ship he was on was too far out to sea. Any rope made of trust had long been broken and was too short to reach Donna or the kids.

Tom came back to the present with the strange awareness that he was shaking his head. He went back to his typing and addressing the issue at hand with his children.

"It recently occurred to me that I never told you how I came to know the Lord. I was not a bad kid. I never did drugs or alcohol or really rebelled against my parents at all. Life for me was fairly simple and unencumbered. I went to school, hung out with my friends, who were good kids, and did odd jobs to get my hands on some spending money. That's about all my life amounted to. My parents took me to church each

Sunday, but nothing seemed to connect there. I felt like I was going to heaven because I was a good kid and my parents were good people.

Then my uncle Brian died of a brain aneurysm. It was all so sudden and unexpected. He was a good guy and always took care of people. I always looked forward to his visits, and he never had anything bad to say about anyone. One day he was at our house, and the next day, my Dad sat me down to tell me my Uncle was gone. It was hard for me to believe. I was a sophomore in high school, and I had never lost anyone close to me before.

At the funeral, the Pastor talked a lot about the kind of guy my Uncle Brian was. He was close to my uncle and nailed it pretty well. Then, he started talking about heaven and how a person got there. He said we all have sin and sin is what keeps us from God. He told us the only way to clear up our sin and get to heaven is by asking Christ to forgive us. I'm not sure that at the time I understood all that he was talking about, but I knew, even though I wasn't a *bad* kid, I needed forgiveness. So that night, as I lay in my bed, I talked to God about it. I asked Him to come into my life and to forgive me of my sins and to change me. I looked around expecting angels, or music, or something. But the room was as silent as it was before I started. Still, I could tell there was something inside of me that had changed. There is no way to explain it to you, but somehow I knew I had been forgiven and I was now different.

This is the part where I could tell you my life skyrocketed into success and all my problems were over, but that didn't happen. In fact, I ran into some problems I hadn't anticipated. The next week, my girlfriend decided that she liked James Lexington more than me so she bid me farewell. A short while after that, one of my best friends moved away. Right on the heels of that I was let go from the summer job I was counting on. And then I lost a money clip that was given to me by my Grandfather. Life wasn't easy. I had every reason to walk away from my new relationship with the Lord. But through all of this, life was still really good. And my faith in the Lord stood the test and got stronger still.

When I was a freshman in college I was away from home and very lonely. My studies weren't going very well, and I felt so isolated. Friday night came and the guys in my dorm were heading out to a fraternity house. I wanted to go along. But the guys knew that I went to church and knew that some of the things going on at the fraternity house wouldn't fit well with my beliefs. So they asked me if I was o.k. with drinking and watching "the show." I wasn't. So in less than a polite way, they suggested I don't go. I was left out.

I went back to my dorm room for a while, but boredom drove me to take a walk. I found myself out by the college lake. The place was dark and completely deserted, which is about the way I felt. So as I walked around the lake, I talked to God. I told Him that I felt alone and left out. I told Him that I felt like I didn't have any real friends and that following Him wasn't easy. In my time out at the lake, I simply poured out my heart to God. Then I waited for Him to respond. This is what some people call a crises of belief. It's a time when you have to decide which way you're going to go with your faith. Are you going to stick with God and trust him through the dark times, or are you going to abandon the faith and go your own way?

I don't know what I was expecting—maybe a visit from some angel or a small voice in the wind, but all was deathly silent. I don't exactly know how, but somehow, I knew God was there. I couldn't see Him, touch Him, or hear Him, but I just knew He was there, and He cared about me. So in that moment, I resolved to follow Him no matter what. I didn't care if I spent my entire college experience alone. I didn't care if people made fun of me, or if they ignored me completely. In that window of time, I decided that I would be faithful to Him regardless of what the world threw at me. I left the lake area with a much lighter heart than when I came."

Tom sat back in his chair. He found his mind drifting back to an episode that occurred one night during his sophomore year in college. He and four other guys were sitting around the lounge area watching T.V. For reasons still unknown, they got into a discussion about religion. Each fellow gave his opinion while Tom listened. They knew he was religious, and they knew he went to church.

Finally one of the guys turned to Tom and said, "Tom, I've never heard what you believe." It seemed like the whole room, and maybe the entire world, turned toward Tom. He wasn't prepared for this and his heart was in his throat. He wasn't ashamed of his faith, but was not accustomed to sharing openly about what he believed. Mostly, he was afraid of saying the wrong thing. He really didn't want to blow it in front of these guys.

With all this on his mind, he took a deep breath and with all the conviction he could muster he simply said, "I believe Jesus is who He said He is. And if Jesus is not who He said he is, then nothing ultimately matters. But if Jesus is who He said He is, He is the only thing that ultimately matters." Tom tried not to look surprised but couldn't really believe that he had encapsulated his beliefs so concisely. He did remember thinking immediately after he voiced that, *That was good! I need to write that down.* The group of guys sat there in silence the way people pause after a shocking movie or stunning news clip, waiting for everything to sink in.

Except for a couple of abbreviated "humms," no one made a sound for a short time until one of the guys said, "Well, anybody want to get some pizza?" That was a moment in time that Tom knew he would never forget. *No turning back. No turning back.*

Tom jumped back to the task at hand. "I'm telling you this so that you will see that I've had my times when I could have walked away from God, but I never did. I never became a fair weather follower of God. Life has not always been easy. I've had my share of difficulties. Obviously, I'm in one now. But knowing that God is ultimately in control has made things so much easier.

I want to share with you what I think are the *big five* of Christian growth. I call them the big five because I believe that if a person will keep these five things in mind, it will go a long way toward helping him stay close to the Lord.

1. Remember that God <u>always</u> answers prayer. It may not be the answer that you're looking for, but He is always listening and always responding. He always has your best interest in mind, and He ultimately wants better things for you than you do. God answers prayers in one of four ways: He says, 'Yes, No, Wait (because the timing is not right) or Yes, and here's more.' The depth of your prayers is a reflection of the depth of your faith. Don't be afraid to ask God for big things—things that if they come to pass, you'll know it is only by the hand of God. Be alert to what you see around you. You'll find that God is always in the process of answering your prayers.

2. There really is strength in numbers. You will become what you surround yourself with. Surround yourself with the right people, and good things will happen. I've made a habit of building good people into my life. Bob is always there for me. He is the picture of loyalty. Jim is steady and assuring. Perry keeps me accountable and is the iron that sharpens me. Tony demonstrates passion for Christ in everything he does. Dave is a man of deep faith and adventure. These guys have helped shape me into everything I am regarding my Christian walk. Make sure you build the right people into your life so that they will influence you to walk in a way that will please the Lord.

3. Never get away from the Christian disciplines. There are certain habits that if you develop them and exercise them,

they will help deepen you in your walk of faith. I believe the key habits for growing Christians are prayer, Bible study, service, fellowship, worship, and giving. These are in no particular order neither should one be done to the exclusion of the other. They are each essential if you're going to be everything God wants you to be.

4. Understand that your life is your witness. You always demonstrate what you believe by what you do. The words need to be said, but if they can't be backed up by your actions, they will grow hollow and have limited impact. We will never be able to estimate the damage so many have done to the Christian faith simply because they have spoken out boldly about particular things, and then been found to violate those same principles.

On a personal note, I have a problem with those in the entertainment industry who want to hold concerts and banquets to benefit worthy causes such as AIDS. They want people to attend, give their time and money and take a stand against this disease. All the while, they are producing movies, singing songs, and living lifestyles that promote the very behavior that spreads AIDS.

Until you demonstrate clearly what you believe by how you live, you will never make the changes in your world you are called to make. It all comes down to obedience. Almost every problem I've had in my life can be routed back to the area of obedience.

When I was just a boy, I found out very quickly that in our home there were certain rules that were not to be violated. I learned very early, as long as I obeyed the rules my parents set up, life generally went very smoothly. But when I disregarded the rules and went my own way, life was not so good. The same is true of a walk with the Lord. When you walk in obedience, He leads you beside the still waters. But when you wander from His path, you find that life becomes much more difficult than it has to be.

5. Regularly reflect back on all the good things God has done for you. There will be times when God has rescued you, protected you, and provided for you. Don't ever forget them. It will take us getting to heaven to fully understand all the times God has intervened on our behalf, but every once in a while, His hand of protection or benevolence is too obvious to miss.

Daniel is a friend of mine from college and lives in another city. His office is on the third floor of their home. One day, his wife left to run a short errand in town. She left their three-year-old son Michael, in the care of Daniel. Michael busied himself with toys while Daniel busied himself with work. Moments later, while Daniel was at his desk, Michael was walking along the work counter. Daniel heard a strange sound and turned to see that Michael was gone and the screen on the window was padding against the pane. The unthinkable had happened. Michael had leaned against the screen and had fallen out the third story window. Daniel rushed from his chair and was outside their home in seconds. He found Michael lying on his back on the concrete sidewalk completely calm, awake, alert, and absolutely unharmed. The ambulance came, and took him to the hospital where he was checked out. No cuts, no broken bones, no bruises, and only one explanation—God.

We've seen God's good hand in our lives too. We moved to a new town just after Madison was born. I took a sizable cut in pay. Because we decided that Mom would stay home after we started a family, we lost her income. The contract on the home we were selling fell through so we were faced with two mortgages at the same time. Needless to say, we were financially strapped. We had made arrangements to pay off the hospital bill from Madison's birth, at the rate of $50 per month. We knew that it would take forever to pay it off, but it really was all we could afford.

One day, I went out to the mailbox and found the monthly bill from the hospital. My heart sank. I didn't have $50. But as I went through the rest of the mail, I found an envelope with no return address. In it was a note that simply said, "God provides." Wrapped in the note was a fifty-dollar bill. God had come through again.

As you go through your life, never forget all the times when God slices through time to bring about something good for you. The world may label all these things a co-incidence, but if your heart is sensitive enough, you will see the hand of God and label them God-incidences.

Four major things that I've noticed about God have kept me close to Him: (1) God loves us. He loves us enough to meet us where we are, but too much to leave us there. It is possible to experience love without experiencing God. But it is not possible to experience God without experiencing love. (2) God is never late. He's never early, but He's never late. His timing is perfect. When God holds back on giving us a blessing, it's because it's not good for us or we're not ready for it. It is never because He's not ready for it. (3) God is never wrong. He doesn't always do things the way we want Him to, but He is never wrong in what He does. The very second God is wrong, or needs a back up plan, He ceases to be God. The very definition of God calls for Him to be perfect. (4) Life is tough, but God is good. You cannot measure God through the lens of life. Everything that comes our way is designed by God not to destroy us but to drive us closer to Him.

With all the above being understood, please grasp my feelings regarding my passing. The end of my life means God has simply made a decision to enjoy a relationship with me up close. I will wait for you! We will be together again! We will laugh again. Life will be better than anything you can imagine! I promise!"

Tom felt a heaviness come over him. At first it felt somewhat like depression but he was quick to realize he was physically tired. He pushed himself from his chair and dropped onto the couch that Marcie had vacated. Sleep came quickly, bringing with it a very strange dream.

As Tom felt himself sink into sleep, he saw himself alone in a field. The sun was shining, the clouds were white and puffy, and the meadow was filled with flowers of every color imaginable. Without warning, a fear came over him. He felt like something was coming although he was completely alone. He began running, and as he ran, he noticed two things happening. The fear began to build, and his ability to run began to wane. As he ran across the meadow, fear turned to panic, and his ability to run from whatever was coming was almost non-existent. He felt as though he was running in glue or syrup. The harder he ran, the thicker it became. Still, the danger loomed ever closer. He felt it advancing toward him like an enemy army about to crest the hill. Tom looked back over and over but never saw anything. Still he knew it was there, and he knew he had to escape. He could almost feel it grabbing him. In a startling instant, he lunged to get away and shook himself awake.

His breathing was heavy and his forehead was covered in sweat. His eyes darted around the room almost expecting to find what was chasing him. Nothing. It was a curiously bad dream. He sat up, shook the fog from his head, and wiped his eyes and brow. He felt he had been asleep for only a few short moments, but the clock told him it was closer to forty-five minutes. This only added to the strangeness of the situation. He made his way to the kitchen and downed a large glass of water. The water was cold, and he could feel it coat his throat and hit his stomach. He hadn't noticed how thirsty he was. He thought, *It must have been all that running*. He slid the glass on the counter and headed for a shower.

TUESDAY, MAY 13

Tom and Marcie were reclining by a lake each immersed in a book. A friend of theirs had given them the gift of a one-night stay at an inn. Even though it was a school night, they were able to farm out the kids and take advantage of the opportunity. It was kind of a spur-of-the-moment thing but they just couldn't pass it up. The packing was swift and the planning was swifter. They enjoyed the two-hour drive up to the lake and talked the entire time. Tom commented on how it felt like they were newlyweds at the front end of their lives together.

It was a beautiful spring day. The air was still with only a small intermittent breeze. Periodically, they would put their books down and take in the surroundings. There were very few boats on the lake which made the water look like glass. The trees were in full bloom, bearing the unique light green they carried at the end of the budding season. Occasionally, a fish jumped to add just enough movement to assure them the world had not completely stopped. Every once in a while, Marcie would hold her book close to her chest and let out an audible sigh. This erased any misgivings Tom may have had regarding the trip. He smiled and thought, *Just what the doctor ordered.* The world in which they were currently living was the right place to be. They would spend the remaining part of the day just drinking in the tranquility and top it off with a breathtaking view of the sunset.

Inside the house they settled in with the rest of the guests for a full home cooked meal. They had decided on the way not to share Tom's medical condition with anyone. They wanted to avoid being the topic of conversation or the focal point of pity. Though the inn was not full, they met several couples that were very pleasant. One couple had been married for over forty years and counted this as their twentieth time at the inn. Another couple was celebrating their second anniversary and looked to Tom and Marcie as if they couldn't have celebrated their fifteenth birthdays. The rest of the guests were cordial and pleasant but were not overly interested in spending a lot of time with anyone else other than the one they were with. Tom and Marcie understood and held them innocent.

After dinner, Tom and Marcie strolled through the dimly wooded trail that linked the house to the main road. The path was about a mile long but the couple walked at a pace that made it seem much longer. They were in no rush. They each were in the company of their best friend. They each understood that time and trial had been a blessing to them rather than a curse, and they communicated well how thankful they were for each other.

A peaceful sleep came upon them without reluctance. As usual, Tom went out first while Marcie rested her head on his chest. For some reason, her mind wandered back to a memory of an episode that happened after about their second year of marriage.

From Marcie's perspective, it was an ordinary Thursday. She and Tom went to work, completed their day and arrived back at home close to the same time. Tom sat in the recliner with the mail in his hands and the paper in his lap, while Marcie rummaged through the fridge for some pizza and salad left over from Tuesday night. The phone rang and Marcie caught it on the second ring. The man on the other end asked for Tom. Marcie figured it had to do with work, and she slid the cordless phone down Tom's chest and into his lap.

He mouthed, "Who is it?" Marcie shrugged and went back to preparing their meal.

"Hello---Yes, this is Tom---Oh, that's all right---Well, I didn't see any other option---That would be great---I appreciate it---Have a good night."

Tom boosted himself from the chair and walked into the kitchen to hang up the phone.

"What was that all about?" Marcie said while sprucing up the salad.

"Well, a funny thing happened to me today at lunch," Tom answered. He leaned his back against the edge of the counter and placed his palms on the top. Marcie continued her work on the salad while Tom began his story. "We had a special presentation by one of our venders at work. They catered a great breakfast so I nibbled a little as he talked. At lunch I went to Bennington's by myself. I thought I was hungrier than I was so when I finished eating what I wanted I asked for a doggie bag. They brought my food back in a box and I planned on splitting that with you tonight.

When I got back to the office, I went to put it in the break room fridge. A couple of the guys stopped me when they saw the box from Bennington's. They begged me to show them what I had in the box. When I opened it up, it was full of cash. Somehow, they had switched the cash box with my doggie box back at the restaurant. I got their cash and they got my steak and ribs combo. The guys in the office went nuts! They counted it out, and it came to over $5,000."

Marcie's mouth dropped open, and she sat down at the table. At that moment, the salad no longer had her attention.

"They asked me what I was going to do with it, and I told them I had to take it back. The guys went ballistic. I told them if I didn't, someone was going to lose his job and I didn't want to go home knowing I could have prevented that. I told them a lifetime of sleeping well beats a garage full of toys any day. George Andrews went with me because he said he had to see the look on the guys face when I gave him the money back. When I returned the money, the manager thanked me and asked for my card. I gave it to him and left. He called the owner of the franchise and that was him who called. He said thanks and invited you and me for a weekend to their corporate getaway."

Tom leaned on the table across from Marcie. "So, how was your day?"

Marcie smiled. "Pretty good. I foiled a bank robbery, rescued a baby from a burning building, and developed a plan for world peace. Same ol, same ol. And if I had heard that story from anybody else, I would have been surprised." She stood up, leaned across the table and planted a strong kiss on his lips. She leaned back, put her hands on her hips and smiled while she slowly shook her head, "Boy, was I smart when I picked you!"

As the silence of the night closed in, she heard the strong beat of the heart of a man whose insides were far bigger than his outsides. She was proud to be his wife. She was blessed to be his friend. She was thankful to be with him. He was her hero and she was his queen. Right here and right now was the best time and place to be where she was.

WEDNESDAY, MAY 14

Tom and Marcie slept in that day then slowly worked their way back home stopping at several small shops as the urges hit them. They did more looking than buying but did manage to purchase a few small pieces of pottery and some home-made peanut brittle. They arrived home shortly before the children and unpacked before the door swung open and the kids piled in. It had only been a couple of days, but each of them somehow felt that Tom and Marcie were gone longer. Hugs and kisses were passed all around and the family hovered over a fresh can of peanut brittle. Tom and Marcie shared their trip followed by the children giving a short version of their day. An hour later the Redden kids headed off to their own corners of the world.

The trip had taken more out of Tom than he noticed so he shuffled his way to the couch for a nap. As he slept, he once again dreamed of being in the meadow. Everything was the same as before. The flowers were beautiful, the grass was green, and the wind was blowing a slight breeze on his face. Then the fear came back. He sensed it deep within and could almost hear it. Closer and closer it approached, and Tom fled. As he ran, his feet got heavier and heavier, and his steps got slower and slower. Whatever was coming was gaining on him. He was in a panic and found himself fighting against gravity and exhaustion. He kept looking back, seeing nothing, but could almost feel it on top of him. As it crushed down upon him Tom dove to the ground shaking him awake.

He was breathing heavily and covered with sweat. Tom sat up and wiped his face with his sleeve. It was so frightening. It all seemed so real. What could it mean? Marcie entered the kitchen while Tom splashed water on his face.

She put her hand on his back. "What happened to you? You're soaking wet."

Tom turned the water off and reached down for a paper towel. He mopped his face and neck and threw the towel into the wastebasket on the other side of the room. "I had a bad dream. It was really weird!" Tom shared the dream with his wife. "But the strangest part of the whole thing is, I've had the same dream one time before. They were almost completely identical. I don't know if it's the medication or what, but something's messing with my head."

Marcie brushed his hair out of his eyes. "I wonder what it means."

"I have no idea. All I know is, it's got me shaken. I hope this is not a sign of things to come."

FRIDAY, MAY 16

The family was sprawled about the living room enjoying pizza and a movie. It was Madison's turn to pick, and she chose a wilderness adventure. The boys made fun of it at first, but then settled in when they noticed it came around to their liking.

When the movie ended, Tom shared with them a fish story. "Did I ever tell you about the time I was trout fishing in Alaska?" No one ever knew why he bothered to ask, because no matter the response, Tom always proceeded to tell the story.

"Well, I was by myself about thigh deep in the stream and fifteen feet from the bank. I had caught a few fish and was having a great day enjoying my surroundings. All of a sudden I heard this awful chatter. I looked down stream and saw a squirrel going absolutely crazy. He was out on a branch that was about half way across the stream. His tail was twitching and popping all over the place, and he was making quite a racket. Then I noticed what was going on. Out in the middle of the stream, about three feet below the branch was a rock. On that rock was a good size acorn. That little fella was going bonkers trying to figure out how to get that acorn. I watched the entire time. Finally the little guy couldn't handle it any more. He dropped down on that rock and grabbed his prize. Then all of a sudden, whoosh! A great big 'ol trout, the biggest one I've ever seen, came out of the water, snatched the squirrel, and disappeared below the surface." The family sat there in silence for about five seconds.

"Then as I watched, I saw the same trout come back up and put another acorn on the rock."

Tom looked down and the family looked stunned.

Then John broke in, "No way! You're lyin'."

The rest of the family joined in and followed their

comments with beatings from their pillows. The next activity was a typical Redden family wrestling match and pillow fight.

SATURDAY, MAY 17

Tom's hand rested on the keyboard. He had so much to say with so little understanding of how much time he had to say it. As always, he wanted it to be meaningful and helpful. He wanted his children to remember not just who he was, but what he stood for and what he believed to be the really important necessities to a successful life. He looked at his outline, took a deep breath, and let his mind dictate what his fingers would do.

#3-BE WISE WITH YOUR MONEY

"What happens to you financially is, in a large part, determined by your perspective regarding money and possessions. Too many people think their value is equated with their stuff. They think that if they have the latest, newest, and most expensive thing on the market it makes them somebody. They have equated money and things with success, significance, and happiness. So as the old adage goes, they buy things they don't need, with money they don't have, to impress people they don't like. In the end, they wind up being slaves to those they borrowed from, and go through so much of their life carrying a heavy burden that keeps them from really enjoying all the great things life has to offer. There will always be something else that you can buy. There is never enough money for all the things that you can purchase. Too many people spend their entire lives straining for the brass ring on the merry-go-round of life. At the end of their life, when they finally get the ring, they find that it's tarnished, and they're just too tired and dizzy to enjoy it.

Please understand this: Your value is not decided by what you live in, drive, or the digits in your bank account. Your value is independent of your wealth or possessions. However, the value you place on them can shape your character, and therein lies your value.

I grew up not far from a man named Doug. I never knew his last name but everyone knew what he was like. Doug didn't have a lot of money or things, but he had a wide reputation of being generous. Whenever anybody needed help, Doug was always there. I believe he could fix virtually anything. He was just one of those guys who was very mechanically inclined. He could help you with your car, lawnmower, dishwasher, or fence. If you needed to borrow anything, and I mean anything, Doug was the man to see. I never once heard about him turning anyone down. He was just that kind of guy.

One day, my dad was putting in a new mailbox. He knew he needed a posthole digger, so he called Doug. Not only did Doug say yes, but he even brought an auger to our house. Doug offered to dig the hole for my father, but my dad assured him he could handle it. While my dad was running the machine, a neighbor two doors down asked if he could borrow it to dig some holes for a deck he was building. My father told him he needed to check with Doug first (you don't lend out the things you borrow). So my father called Doug, and as expected, Doug said yes. When the neighbor was done, he brought it back to our house, and my father and I went to Doug's and returned it.

My dad thanked him enthusiastically, but Doug just shrugged it off. 'I never met someone as generous with his stuff as you are,' my dad said.

Doug just looked back at my dad and said kind of shyly, 'Listen. I learned a long time ago, that I'm just a manager of all the Lord gives me.'

What an attitude! What a perspective! Doug is a guy who gets it! He understands that it's more important to own things than to have your things own you.

On the other hand, there was an old man who lived about two blocks away from where we lived when I was a boy. His name was Mr. Manebach. He was mean, and angry, and I don't know anybody who liked him. He lived alone, and no one ever bothered to ask him for anything because we were all so sure that the answer would be a loud *No!* The adults didn't have anything to do with him, and all the kids were scared to death of him. Timmy Doherty told me that he ate children and that if you looked him straight in the eye, he could hypnotize you and make you come into his house where you would be killed and eaten.

I didn't believe him, but just to be sure, every time I went passed his house, whether on my bike or walking, I always made it a point to travel on the other sided of the road, and I never once looked him straight in the eye. As best as I can remember, his was the only house we skipped when we trick or treated. For the most part, the entire neighborhood just avoided him.

Late one summer afternoon, I was over at my buddy Bill Meyer's house. Bill lived about four blocks away, but we spent a lot of time together. We were playing hard, and somehow I lost all track of time. When I asked Bill's Mom for the time, I found I was late, very late, for dinner. Using a combination of walking and running, I tore off for home. I used every short cut I could think of. At the next corner was Mr. Manebach's house. As I got closer and closer to his house, I debated whether or not to take the ultimate chance and cut across his back yard. I went for it. I cleared the short hedge with ease and put my legs in another gear I didn't know I had.

From out of nowhere, the old man appeared. How was that possible? Could he have been waiting for me the whole day? I tried to avoid him, but I was moving too fast. I made a turn and fell, sliding across the wet grass and stopping just inches from him. I scrambled to my feet, but it was too late. He had me. The back of my t-shirt was knotted up in his hand and he jerked me toward him.

'You're on my property!' he yelled. 'No one comes on my property! You understand?' Of course I understood. In fact, at that moment, I understood that better than anything any ten-year old could understand. But I never got to tell him that. Before I knew what was going on I was seated in a hardback chair in his kitchen writing my phone number down. In minutes, my father was there. Mr. Manebach scolded my father like he was a junior high kid. My Dad assured him I meant no harm and had me apologize.

On the front porch, my father told me to start walking home and that he would catch up. I went down the steps and slowly walked down the driveway. I wanted to hear what my Father had to share with this mean old man. I waited around the side of the bushes and could hear and see it all.

'Listen, Mr. Manebach. I know you're upset about your precious lawn. I told you my son wouldn't do that again. But now let me tell you something. That's my boy. And he means a lot more to me than your silly yard means to you. So let me make something perfectly clear.'

Then I saw my Dad take his index finger and poke Mr. Manebach in the chest several times for emphasis. 'If you ever put your filthy hands on my boy again, I'm gonna bury you in your own yard.' With that he stepped off the porch and stepped on the small shrub that grew near the steps. He walked straight across the yard and grabbed my hand as he stepped off the driveway. As we walked along, I'll never forget his words.

'Tom, you were wrong. But he was more wrong." Then he put his arm around my shoulder as he said, "Now let's go get some supper.'

The summer after my junior year in college, I was

talking to my father about that incident. I asked him whatever happened to Mr. Manebach. He told me he had died a couple of years before. Then he leaned into me and said, 'But you and I know that he really died about thirty years before that.' He said he didn't even have a funeral because no one would be there. The funeral home just buried him in one of their plots and nobody really knows where it is.

That's the way it is when your things matter more to you than people. It's very easy to lose perspective and think that things will bring you happiness. But it makes for a sad and lonely life and can even lead you into making some very poor decisions.

Just two weeks ago, there was a scandal that reached statewide proportions. The CEO of a rather large investment firm was indicted for stealing from the company. He pleaded guilty but will have to pay a huge fine and spend a good bit of his life in jail. I'll never forget his comment about the entire event. He said, 'I guess I lost perspective on how much was enough.'

When you know how much is enough, then you can relax after you've gotten there. You'll have so much more to give, and you won't spend your time chasing another dollar. My friend Rob understands this. He's not a millionaire, but he is very well off. He's worked hard in his career and done well financially. One day over lunch, he told me that he had made enough money for him and his family to live on for the rest of their lives. Now he just works so that he can make money to give away. He mentioned that as a young boy his father taught him that there were three things that he needed to do with money: save some, spend some, and give some away. He said he's been exercising that principle his entire life and it's made all the difference in the world. Then he told me that of those three things, he's enjoyed giving money away more than anything else. He only shared with me, (reluctantly), a few of the things that he gave his resources to. Among the things that he sponsors are a scholarship to the university, five children to go to the camp for mentally challenged kids, the resource room at the senior adult center, and the furniture for a house for "habitat for humanity" each year. He is free to do all this simply because he understands how much is enough.

The way you understand how much is enough is by seeing the difference between a want and a need. Too often we blur the lines between these two. We think just because we want certain things badly, it is a need in our life. Needs in your life are things like a reliable car, proper clothing, good food and water, and other things that you understand are essential to life. The way you figure out what needs and what wants are is to simply ask yourself this question: What happens if I don't get it? If the answer is nothing, or I'll be disappointed, then what you're dealing with is a want and not a need. Understanding the distinction between the two will save you a lot of pain and trouble.

This leads to another important principle. Never spend more than you make. This is called living within your means, and it's becoming more and more rare these days. I've tried to teach you the concept of 'deferred gratification.' If you will put off what you want and wait until you can afford it, you'll find you can enjoy it much more than if you have it and also have a great debt that goes along with it. Often times the item you *had* to have is outlived by the debt you acquired in getting it. Always remember the adage, 'Debt is fun to acquire, but hard to retire.' Real freedom is not found in running out and spending every time the urge hits you. Real freedom is found in discipline!

If you will be disciplined in the area of your finances, you will avoid the burden that always comes with assuming a large amount of debt. We are so glad we decided not to spend our money on the latest trinkets that came down the pike. A long time ago, we made the decision to invest our money in family memories. We saved up money each year so we could freely enjoy a vacation together. We've gone to concerts, shows, ballgames, and movies. But never once did we go into debt to do those things. And because of that discipline, we were free to sit back and enjoy a worry-free experience together.

Remember where your money comes from in the first place. It comes from God. You have what you have simply because God has blessed you with it. So in turn, you need to give to the work of the Lord. The Bible tells us to give of our first fruits. That means the first place you give is to God. Your Mom and I always write our first check each month to the ministries of the church. I learned this while I was just a little boy and would watch my dad write his check and place it in the plate at church on Sunday. He never drew attention to it, but he never missed a time of giving.

We were sitting on the front porch one summer evening, enjoying the sunset, and somehow we started talking about money. I knew that we were not well off, but also understood, all our needs were met. (I never really went without any of the essentials.) Still money was somewhat tight, and I was often told no to a lot of the extra things that I wanted. I remember asking my dad why he always gave to the church.

Without hesitating, (it seemed like he'd settled this in his mind a long time ago), he told me, 'I give to the Lord's work for five reasons: (1) It's a command. (2) It brings God satisfaction when His children trust Him enough to honor him with their resources. God loves it when we give, even when it's hard and things are tough. (3) When I give, I get to be part of the ministry my money goes toward. It sort of gets credited to my account. (4) Giving always brings a sense of pride and joy to the giver. (5) God honors those who honor Him. This includes the area of giving.' Then he turned to me and said, 'God shovels in and I shovel out. His shovel's bigger, and He started first.'

There will always be the temptation to chase easy money.

You can waste a lot of time and money on get-rich-quick schemes. Remember, if it sounds too good to be true, it usually is."

Tom paused for a moment. This was a lesson he learned the hard way. He and Marcie had only been married a couple of years when he got an *inside tip* from a co-worker on a stock that was poised to go through the roof. The guy seemed to know what he was talking about. He bragged about how he had successfully invested in several stocks, and it looked like he had all the material things to back up his claims. He drove a new car, had a good size house, and always vacationed in exotic places. As it turned out, all these things were merely a facade, and he was, in fact, up to his neck in debt. But this stock was going to go big, and it was going to go fast. It was a penny stock and was offered at $.79 a share. It was projected to go to $8 within three months, and everyone in Tom's office was jumping on the bandwagon.

Tom couldn't resist. He put down $2,000 of their money and waited for the gravy train to pull up. He didn't tell Marcie (a huge mistake) because he wanted to come home and surprise her by laying out some cash and making her so proud of her financially savvy husband. He stood to make over $18,000, and while he waited for the stock to skyrocket, he dreamed of all the things they would do with the money: A down payment on a larger home, a new car, a big vacation, dining at the best restaurant, a college fund. Tom's mind bounced from one great idea to another while he checked the papers each day.

Then the anticipated move happened. Slowly, but surely, the stock started to climb. In one day, it went from $.79 to .89. A couple of days later it was at $1.02. By the end of two weeks, it had jumped to $1.20. The office was going crazy. It seemed all anybody talked about was the rapid growth of the office baby. It was the only thing that mattered. Tom tried to concentrate on his work but found it harder and harder as the stock rose. A week later it was at $1.32. People were spending their stock money before they cashed in their shares. Tom was in the midst of a financial frenzy. He had heard about people hitting it big in the stock market but never thought he would be a part of it. And he wasn't. As fast as the rocket took off, it ran out of steam and plummeted to earth. Everyone's heart, including Tom's, was sick to watch the stock drop from $1.32 to $1.11, to $.93, to $.65, to $.34, to worthless.

Tom's hopes and dreams were below the level of the stock. Losing all that money was hard. But it wasn't as hard as going home and telling Marcie about what he had done. She was angry, and she was disappointed. It wasn't so much the loss of money that bothered her. What really hurt was Tom never told her about his plans. She should have been a part of it.

Back at the keyboard, Tom raised his chin and shook his head. He learned a hard lesson that didn't need to be repeated. He pounded the keyboard with these words:

"Be patient with your money. Get lots of advice before you invest in anything, even if it seems like a sure thing. Do the math and figure out the odds. If you start at age 16, and invest $2,000 a year (summer money) in a tax free IRA and do that for four years, by the time you are ready to retire, you will have over $1,000,000. Now that takes time, discipline, and patience. But the reward at the end is worth all the struggle at the beginning.

Money and how you handle it can be a point of great satisfaction or it could be your undoing, making your life miserable. So keep these principles in mind when you're considering the proper use of money:

#1 Know that your value does not increase or decrease with your possessions.

#2 Money and things are not synonymous with success and happiness.

#3 Decide how much is enough and don't waver.

#4 Save some, spend some, and give some away.

#5 Understand the difference between a want and a need.

#6 Live within your means. Never spend more than you make.

#7 Give to God of your first fruits.

#8 Avoid get-rich-quick schemes.

If you will let these principles guide your life, you will do well financially and you will find that everything you own, you truly own, and nothing you own, owns you. That is financially freedom. That is financial success. That is the way to live!"

Tom wheeled his chair around and slid across the floor all in the same motion indicating he had done this hundreds of times before. He was through the door before the chair came to rest. Moves like that forced him to fight to accept the reality of his condition. He went to the kitchen for some flavored coffee. Above him he could hear one of the kids banging around in his room and tried to decide who it was and how long he had been up. It wasn't particularly early nor was it very late. He decided it was Matty, the one who normally rose early. Usually, he could feel the draining effects of putting his thoughts on paper, but somehow this morning he still felt strong and alert enough to continue. He grabbed his favorite mug, the one that had a fat man in a Speedo flexing his muscles. The caption read, *Proud to be the World's Most Humble Man.* He had always gotten a chuckle out of the oversized cup and remembered winning it in the *white elephant* gift exchange at a neighborhood Christmas party. He and Marcie had contributed a video rental card but Tom thought they had gotten the better end of the exchange. While he filled his cup, he thought about what they would give next year. Then he remembered....

Back at his desk, Tom held the mug in both hands and blew the steam from the coffee. Once again, he gazed at the outline and gathered his thoughts. He took a careful sip and dove back into his task.

#4-INVEST IN PEOPLE'S LIVES

People had always been important to Tom. He enjoyed being around people and always tried his best to help them in any way he could. This was a topic about which Tom had no trouble in gathering his thoughts. This was also a topic that his kids would have no trouble remembering times when their Dad put his lessons into practice.

"People have the ability to be your greatest point of fulfillment, or the greatest drain of your emotional energies. They can build you up and make your life amazingly fulfilling or they can tear you down and draw you to a point of deep discouragement.

I've been blessed to have so much of my life filled with the former and very little of it surrounded by the latter. My Dad was a great example of a person who understood this. He always had time for people and made it a point to let them tell their story whenever they wanted. He taught me, the most precious thing a person possesses is his name. That's why he worked so hard at remembering peoples' names. I've even seen him address someone by name that I know he had only met once and hadn't seen since the first time he was introduced."

Tom leaned away from the keyboard and reflected on a time when he was just seven years old. He and his Dad were at the grocery store. At one end of the juice aisle, his Dad knelt down and pulled Tom close. Turning young Tom around, he pointed to the other end of the aisle. He said, "Tommy, do you see that man with the white shirt and blue cap on?" Tommy nodded. "That's Mr. Ardsley. He's one of the finest men you'll ever get to meet. We served together on the school board before his wife got sick. I want to introduce you to him. Now when I introduce you, shake his hand firmly and look him in the eye and let him know it's nice to meet him. That's what real men do."

Tommy met Mr. Ardsley and followed his Father's instructions fully. He remembered Mr. Ardsley's comment on what a fine young man he was and how impressed he was with his handshake. Tom never forgot the feeling of pride that he carried with him that day. His Dad had often told him, "No one gets a second chance to make a first impression." Today he got to live out that idea.

Back at the monitor, Tom continued his task. "Remember part of our family philosophy: 'People are more important than things.' If you want to be successful in life, stop spending all your time in gathering things and begin spending your time in gathering people. Those who are easy to live with, will be easy to laugh with. Those who are hard to live with, will teach you the fine art of developing a loving attitude.

I remember when we first came up with the concept of a family philosophy. Your Mom and I wanted to find a way to put down on paper what our family stood for. There were two things we wanted you to have a good handle on. We wanted you to have a strong faith in God, and we wanted you to develop a strong love for people.

We knew we were getting through to you with our philosophy when we were visiting friends in their home that was under construction. Matty was a toddler, and John was just four years old. We were talking with the owners, and all the kids were running throughout the house. The sub-flooring was down, and somehow John had scraped his foot against a board and had a very small cut. John came up to us and interrupted us by asking for a *band aid*. I looked at the cut briefly and told him that I would get him one in a minute. We went back to our conversation only to be interrupted again by John. Again, I said, 'In a minute.' John stood there with all the patience a four-year-old boy could muster. Finally, he patted me on the hand and said, 'People matter more than things and I need a band aid.' I understood that he understood and got him what he needed.

The entire world seems to be scrambling to make a living. As important as that is, it is not the most important thing that you can do. The most important thing that you can do is not found in making a living; it's found in making a difference. That's where you build memories. That's where you establish a reputation. And the way you make a difference is by investing in peoples' lives.

A popular slogan that seems to be running people's lives is, 'He who dies with the most toys wins.' That seems like a fun idea, but the truth of the matter is, he who dies with the most toys is still dead, and in the fight for toys, his soul probably died a few years before his body. The fact is, the best things in life are not things at all. No, the real issue is not things. The real issue is people, and he who dies with the most friends will feel like a winner his entire life.

I've been to enough funerals to know that at the end of a person's life, no one cares about his title. No one talks about their office or their toys. What people talk about is his character and how that was fleshed out in the way they dealt with people. Words like, generous, kind, loving, friendly, caring, helpful, and faithful all come to the front when someone who has passed on is fondly remembered."

Tom clicked over to his screen of notable quotables. He had one that would be perfect for this point, and he wanted to make sure that he got it right, and he gave the author credit. His screen jumped to the files, and he easily found the topic, "People." About midway down the screen, he saw what he was looking for. He pasted the quote to his manuscript. "People will forget what you said, and people will forget what you did, but people will never forget how you made them feel." Maya Angelou. *How true that is,* Tom thought as his mind wandered once again to an event that happened about five years ago.

Tom had taken their car in to get the battery tested. He had been having trouble getting it started and hoped it was something as simple as needing a new battery. When it was his turn to be waited on, he read the shirt label revealing it would be Wally that would be taking care of him. If appearances were any indication, Wally was of retirement age. He asked a few questions and then rounded up a cart carrying tools and a diagnostic machine. Within minutes Wally had determined the battery needed replacement. Tom bought a battery and asked for some tools to replace his old one. With a hand, Wally waved him off. "That's my job. I'll have you up and runnin' in no time at all." Because of the corrosion on the old battery, the job took close to an hour. But Wally never backed off and never showed any signs of impatience. He did a great job and made Tom feel like he was the only customer the store would have all day. Tom was so impressed with Wally that on Monday he wrote a letter to the store manager complimenting him on hiring Wally and encouraging him to do everything he could to keep him.

On the heels of this memory came one about Mr. Wright. He was Tom's ninth grade physical education teacher. He was an athletic man, and although he was probably in his late fifties, he seemed to have the energy of a twenty-year-old. He was always the official pitcher, quarterback, referee, scorekeeper, cheerleader, and disciplinarian.

Everyone seemed to like Mr. Wright but the word was out. Life generally went well in Physical Education as long as you stayed within the parameters of Mr. Wright's rules. He could be your greatest ally, or he could turn into someone you would do well to avoid. Tom liked his teacher and because he tended to comply with Mr. Wright's rules, he generally enjoyed his time in class. He looked up to the man and even thought about what it would be like to someday teach Physical Education like Mr. Wright. Then one day, Tom witnessed an action that brought an entire new level of respect for his teacher.

Kenny was a classmate of Tom's. Because he was short and overweight, he was forced to endure more than his share of ridicule by some of the other kids. They called him names, knocked his books out of his hands, and were certain to choose him last. In the cafeteria, the period before, things had not gone well for Kenny. Somehow he had spilled his entire plate of spaghetti. The sauce had stained him clear through to the t-shirt that he planned on wearing to P.E. When everyone dressed out and lined up, quick attention was drawn to Kenny's shirt. Names like *Messaholic, Grease ball*, and *Pasta Boy* were hurled at him with all the enthusiasm of a dodge ball game. Kenny just stood in line and took it. Tom understood it was wrong and wanted to do something about it but his fear of the kids turning their attention toward him overrode his desire to do what was right, so he just stood in the back of the line in silence. When he entered the gym, Mr. Wright heard the comments. Tom knew Mr. Wright would put a quick halt to all the belittling that was going on. But instead of addressing the class, he went back into his office. That seemed really odd to Tom.

Then Tom saw what was going on. From where he was standing, Tom could see into the locker room. The reflection off the class in the outside door gave him a clear eye into what was going on in the office. He watched as Mr. Wright opened the door to the small fridge on the counter. He saw him pull out a bottle of ketchup and pour some into a paper towel. Then he smiled as he watched him smear it on the front of his t-shirt. The room fell silent when Mr. Wright re-appeared in the gym. He stood in front of the class and looked down at his shirt, "Sorry about my shirt. Accidents happen." Then he looked directly at Kenny, tossed a clean t-shirt at him and winked. That day, Mr. Wright became more than a favorite teacher of Tom's. He became a hero.

Life changed for Kenny too. With puberty, and a weight lifting program on the horizon, he grew taller and his body recomposed itself. He went on to do well in football and even played at a small college in Pennsylvania where he majored in computer technologies. Tom often wondered if it was all due to the way Mr. Wright made Kenny feel that day.

Back on the screen came the words: "We always have a chance to make someone feel better about themselves. I remember a girl I met when I was a Freshman in college. Her name was Maureen. She was from Virginia, and we met during freshmen orientation. She seemed nice and was pleasant to talk with. She carried some extra weight, wore thick glasses, and had long stringy hair. Serious acne had taken its toll on her face leaving marks and small scars. Some of the less sensitive guys had joked about her face being on fire and someone tried to stomp it out with golf spikes. I don't think anybody said that directly to her, but I'm sure she overhead their comments. People can be cruel that way.

During the second week of school, I attended a campus-wide Bible study. I showed up by myself and wasn't sure if I'd know anybody there. When I looked across the circle, I saw Maureen. After the meeting I said *hi*, and we went our separate ways. I saw her at the next several meetings as the group began to get more and more cohesive. About the fifth meeting, I happened to notice that Maureen was absent. I didn't think much of it, but a few days later I ran into her outside the cafeteria. All I said was, "Hey Maureen. We missed you at Bible study the other night." She said thanks and that was the end of it. She came back to Bible study, and I never gave it a second thought.

Then at graduation, she came up to me out of the crowd and said, 'I've got to tell you something. Back in our Freshman year, I bumped into you outside the cafeteria. You told me that I was missed at Bible study. You'll never know how much that meant to me. I was seriously thinking of dropping out of school and maybe life altogether. The fact that someone noticed me and actually missed me was exactly what I needed to hold on a little longer. Thanks!' Then she gave me a quick hug and walked away toward her Mom and Dad. I never saw her again, but she gave me a lesson that I'll never forget. I had a chance to change someone's life, and I took it. It cost me nothing but was as valuable as the diploma I received."

Tom thought of all the people that had invested in his life and had given him everything that he needed to be strong and to face all the challenges that came his way, including and especially the one that was staring him in the face. He drifted back to Dr. Biner, his college adviser. Having been at the school for over twenty-five years, Dr. Biner was an experienced professor in the business department. He was a slight man who walked in a bent over manner due to a degenerative spinal problem. Although he experienced a moderate amount of pain, he never complained and never let it slow him down. He was known for his wisdom as well as his quick wit, and he always seemed to have a pipe in his hand that added to his reputation as a wise man.

While Tom was away from home, Dr. Biner became a secondary father to him. He spent time with Tom and gave him the guidance he needed to negotiate his way through college life. Tom could always count on Dr. Biner for solid advice on a variety of subjects ranging anywhere from study habits to interpersonal relationships.

During Tom's sophomore year, he was pining to Dr. Biner about a girl he was attracted to but didn't seem interested in him. Dr. Biner listened and then looked Tom in the eye and said words that Tom never forgot, "God always gives the best to those who leave the choice to Him." When it was time to find a job, Tom remembered his solid advice, "Don't get too hung up on the salary. The key is to find a job that you can naturally develop a passion for. Avoid looking for a job that you can live with. Find a job that you think you can't live without." After Tom graduated, he still kept in touch with his advisor and always appreciated his fatherly advice and encouragement.

He remembered Mr. Howard, his fourth grade teacher, who told him, "Tom, you only live once, but if you live right, once is enough." There was his Mom and Dad, who in so many ways told him that he could be anything he wanted to be. And Mrs. Morgan, a middle aged woman who lived across the street and always had something from the oven to share. She told him, real winners are people who never give up. Then she lived it out by running a road race two years after diabetes took her lower leg. Name after name and face after face came to Tom's mind as he opened the mental files of all the people who had been involved in his life in some way or another. This drove the peg home that convinced him more than ever that life is about people. It's about investing in their lives and letting them invest in your life in turn.

"What's it all come down to? Our lives are meant for more than just an oxygen/carbon dioxide exchange. We are meant to be involved with all sorts of people in all sorts of ways. You can take a stick that is only a ¼ of an inch thick and snap it with no problem. But take six of those sticks and you'll wear yourself out trying to break them. The strength of plywood lies in the fact that it is made up of thin sheets of wood that are laid on top of one another in a criss-crossed fashion. That's how we find strength in our lives. It's by being together and intertwining our lives with the lives of others that we find strength. Stick with the right people, and they will build you up and help you to be strong."

Tom smiled the smile of a man giving a lesson to others while at the same time knowing he would soon have to live this lesson as he had never done before. This realization caused him to tilt his head to the side and give a slight nod. He hit the save button and went into the living room to see who was stirring.

Tom sat across from Matty and watched him make short work of a bowl of cereal. He was still in his nightclothes and his hair gave evidence that he had not yet seen himself in the mirror that morning. Tom scratched his arm and asked a question of the youngest member of the Redden family. "Matty, it's been a long time since I was a ten-year-old. What does a ten-year-old boy dream about?"

Matty didn't look up. He just tilted his head to the side, shrugged his shoulders and made sounds that if he would have opened his mouth would have said, "I don't know."

Tom scratched his forearm again. "C'mon Matty. If you could do anything, or be anything, or go anywhere, what would it be? What do you daydream about?"

Matty flicked the end of his spoon sending it completely around the bowl and leaned on his elbow. "I guess sometimes, I think about going to the Super Bowl and scoring a touchdown. Then I would have my name in the paper and my picture on T.V. and I could buy all the stuff I wanted."

"Is that all?" Tom asked.

"I also wish I could invent a smart pill so that all you would have to do would be take it and it would make you really smart so that you didn't have to go to school anymore."

Tom scratched the other arm and lean forward. "Anything else?"

"Nope. That's it. Except that sometimes I dream about being really strong so that I could beat up Brendan Guinness. He's always pickin' on somebody, and nobody stops him 'cause he's the biggest kid in the school. That's because he started school late and got left back one time."

"Good for you Matty. Good for you," Tom said as he tussled Matty's hair.

He looked down as he scratched his arm to see red blotches in various parts of his lower arm. Just looking at them made them itch even more. The blotches weren't on any other part of his body, and he didn't itch anywhere else. It was just the insides of his forearms. *Wow. I guess this is a side effect from the infusion,* he thought. *Sure took it a long time to show up. I'll have to let Matt and the folks down at the clinic know about it*. He got up and headed for the bathroom to get some cream. Just minutes after applying the cream, the itching stopped. He was scheduled to go to the clinic later that morning to have more blood drawn, but decided that he ought to write it down anyway.

At the clinic, the nurse looked at his arms and made a note on his chart. Then a nurse who was in charge of his records came in and checked his arms out. Next, a physician's assistant came in and looked his arms over. They all asked the same basic questions. "How long have you had this rash? What did you do to help it? Have you ever had a rash like this before? Have you been outside working around anything you might be allergic to?"

Lastly, the doctor entered and asked to see his arms. *Don't these people ever talk to each other?* Tom thought as he breathed deeply and rolled his eyes. The doctor noted the rash on his own pad and gave him a prescription he could use if it got any worse.

Tom and Marcie left the clinic and motored over to an old restaurant that they favored. It was called *The Stone Gate Inn.* The building was over 100 years old and was made almost entirely of stone. The stone entrance was massive and stately. The cobblestone sidewalk was lined with flowers and wound around the side of the building. The front door was at the top of three steps that had large pools filled with gold fish on either side. Upon entering the foyer, you were met by enormous support beams and beautiful wood veneer. The decorations were lovely and tastefully done, fitting the setting of the house. Tom and Marcie's favorite place to eat was downstairs in the wine cellar. The basement had been converted to a dining area but still kept the coolness and rustic look of a basement. It was dimly lit and carried a natural spring that ran along the far wall. The tables were made of rough wood, giving visitors the idea that maybe they were used in the original building. It was easy to see why this place was one of their favorites. They were seated by a small, unlit fireplace and gave their drink orders to the waitress. Marcie excused herself and went back upstairs to locate the ladies room. Tom watched her form as she walked away. He almost said aloud, *I can't believe I got her.*

His mind traveled back to their earlier days of dating. On their third date, Tom thought it would be fun to rent mopeds in town and tour the countryside. Marcie agreed and a half hour later, they were speeding around on the motorized bikes. They went through the campus and around the park. They found an old covered bridge and stopped long enough to take a few pictures. They sped across a field and through a trail in the woods.

At one point, Marcie was a good bit in front of Tom. The trail came to a fork and she stopped to make a decision. Tom never saw her. Wanting to catch up, he flew down the trail. At the last moment, she came into view. He skidded sideways and their bikes crashed together. He was thrown over her bike and into the briars. His moped landed on top of her, burning her leg with the muffler. The date ended with an unplanned trip to the emergency room. Along with the burn, Marcie's little finger was broken and her thigh was bruised. Tom faired much better. Except for a small gash from a rock and some scrapes from the briars, he was relatively unhurt. Marcie was a good sport about it, but Tom secretly wondered if there would be a fourth date. For many years afterward, whenever the subject came up, Marcie would interject in a good natured sort of way, how much she loved Tom even though he tried to kill her by throwing a moped at her.

Tom claimed to have salvaged their dating relationship and unbeknownst to him their entire future together by making quick arrangements for another date. By way of conversation he learned that she loved the theatre. In particular, she was attracted to musicals. Through research, he found a place just outside of Greensboro. It was a dinner theatre and just the thing Tom needed to put their last dating debacle in the distant past.

While Marcie was occupied with mending, Tom was busy making plans for a great night. A week later, Tom asked Marcie to keep the following Saturday night free. She agreed but wanted to know where they were headed. He told her it was a secret but guaranteed that it would be both great and safe.

He picked her up at 5:00 p.m., still not telling her where they were going. Not until they reached the drive for the theatre did she figure out their destination. "You may have just redeemed yourself Mr. Redden." He smiled but made no reply. They entered and were seated and given instruction for the buffet. The food was delicious and the atmosphere was just right. The play they enjoyed was a musical comedy titled, *There's no place like Rome*. It was well performed and presented in good taste. On the way back to the car, Marcie put her arm (the one without the splinted finger) in Tom's and whispered, "Redemption complete."

Tom pumped his hand and whispered rather loudly, "Yes!"

Marcie returned from the restroom followed by the waitress with their drinks. They enjoyed over an hour of conversation and a hearty lunch. Before leaving the table, Marcie commented, "Tom, I've come to a conclusion. I've decided that six weeks with you is worth more than six years with any other man." She reached out and kissed him strongly yet gently on the lips. Tom could only picture himself as the most fulfilled man on earth.

He touched Marcie's cheek and said, "I know that God doesn't play favorites, but having you as my wife makes me believe that if He did, I would be one of them." They ate their meal slowly and held hands as they worked their way out the door and through the parking lot.

When they arrived home, Tom felt fatigued. He laid down for a nap and slept soundly for two hours. The only problem was, it was a two and a half hour nap. Somewhere during that last fifteen minutes, the dream came back. It was just like all the others: The meadow, the sunshine, the tall grass, the flowers, the pursuit, and the fear. Tom remembers that during the dream, he told himself it was a dream and that he shouldn't be afraid. He even remembers remarking that he would wake up soon. None of that reasoning stemmed the fear that came upon him. He awoke by Marcie's shaking him. He was sweating and breathing heavily.

She sat down on the edge of the couch and brushed his hair from his forehead. "Same dream?" she asked.

"Yeah" he said, turning to his side and hugging a throw pillow. "It was almost identical to the others. Even the emotions were the same. I try to fight it, but the fear just leaps on me like before. I wish I knew what it meant."

She continued to stroke his hair. "I wish I could help you." She got up and brought back a glass of water. Tom sat up and drank his water. They sat there in silence while Marcie rubbed his back. After a few minutes, Tom stood up feeling better. "I'm going to take a shower and maybe write a little bit. I think that will calm me down some."

After the shower, Tom stared at the console and gathered his thoughts.

#5-NEVER STOP LEARNING

"Some day your formal education will end. Resist the temptation to conclude all your learning is over. It is not! If you do it right, you will be able to continue to learn your entire life. The books you read, the people you meet, the places you go, the experiences you have, all add to your knowledge base and keep life from getting boring and routine.

Books: Knowledge is power. Read, read, read! Each year, I challenge myself to read 24 books. When I first started doing that, I was a little intimidated. But I never had a problem with it, and most years I read many more than the 24 I had planned. Besides the courses I took for my masters in marketing and my regular studies at work, I've read books about nature, leadership, marriage, fatherhood, parenting, biographies, finance, religion, history, and an assortment of novels. I've found it's made me a much more rounded person. I have more confidence and can often easily enter into a conversation in various circles.

People: Sometimes people don't want to learn. With knowledge comes responsibility. And with responsibility comes the possibility of failure. Sometimes people don't want to learn because they are simply afraid of failure.

Understand that wisdom and knowledge are not the same thing. Knowledge is the ability to gain facts. Wisdom is the ability to take those facts and apply them to your life. Knowledge is the *what?* of life. Wisdom is the *so what?* of life.

I went to grade school, middle school, and high school with a boy named Scott. Scott was a genius, and we all knew it. He always got the best grades in the class, and his college board scores were through the roof. But even though Scott had all that knowledge, he was deeply lacking in wisdom. He couldn't carry on a decent conversation, he constantly made bad decisions socially, and he was a poor judge of people. After college, he should have owned his own company, but his inability to put it all together forced him to work toward the bottom of middle management for someone else. He was a clear example of a person who had it all in his head but could never get it to come out to his hands and feet.

On the other hand, I've got a friend named Tony. Tony never made it out of eighth grade. He had to go to work because his father died, and he had to support his Mom and three sisters. Tony knows auto mechanics. He can fix anything inside or outside of a car. If you bring in a car that he's not familiar with, which is rare, he will go home, look it up, and find a way to fix whatever is wrong with it. Not only does he know how to fix it, but he also has the ability to talk you through fixing it yourself. Now that takes talent. That's wisdom.

You know Paul. He's the delivery driver for our company. Paul only has a high school diploma, but when you talk to him, you think that you're talking to a college professor. He has a great command of the English language, and because he is a veracious reader, he can talk to you on just about any subject. He's been in the same business for over thirty-three years and has built up so much vacation and sick time, he could go home today and draw a paycheck for the next three years. Just about every time I talk to him I learn something new. He's given me some insight on all sorts of topics ranging from finances, to politics, to history, to entertainment. I just love talking to the guy. Every time I spend some time with him, I walk away feeling that I'm just a little smarter than I was before.

Then there's my buddy Doug. Doug is one of the kindest, gentlest men I know. He's also one of the wisest. He is great with his hands and is one of those guys that can fix virtually anything. He's good with his mind as well as his hands. He always seems to have the right thing to say at the right time. People, including me, go to Doug because he has a wise way of approaching matters. He's not quick with an answer, but when the answers do come, they come in a way that makes sense to everyone involved.

The key is to surround yourself with people who have wisdom and experience and never be afraid to ask questions. The number one requirement to learning is the willingness to be humble enough to admit your lack of knowledge. Be willing to ask questions and search out answers. By asking questions you become a good conversationalist. People like to talk about themselves and consider it an honor to be recognized for what they know. Invite them to talk about themselves and the areas in which they are interested. You'd be amazed at how much you can learn from people and how quickly they will be drawn to you when you simply ask them about themselves. Because I've gotten to know people and haven't been afraid of asking questions, I've been exposed to woodcarving, welding, farming, and ballroom dancing.

Places: You know that as a family, we've traveled a good bit. Your Mom and I have saved up each year to take you kids to different places both for fun and for learning. We've been to lots of places including D.C., New York, California, Hawaii, as well as an assortment of plays and museums. Our goal has been to expose you to as many different places and as many different things as possible.

Not long ago, I read about a man named Brent. Brent was a successful car salesman. He and his wife were married about eight years before they had their first child. Two years later they had their second child. A third child came along three years after that. Somewhere in the midst of their oldest child going to seventh grade Brent had had enough of the corporate world. He wanted out. They were also disillusioned with the school system and decided to home school their children. Basically, they dropped out of society for two years and went on a learning spree. He sold the business at an enormous profit, and they liquidated all their assets, including their home.

Then they made plans for two years of travel. He and his wife home schooled the three kids in hotel rooms around the world, with heavy doses of visits to all the places they studied. They canoed the Amazon, rode bikes along the Great Wall of China, played hide and seek in the Pyramids, and evaluated the artwork in the Louvre. They studied animals in Africa while on safari and hiked in the Swiss Alps and Machupichu. They toured the Holy Land and floated in the Dead Sea. They found themselves in volcanoes, igloos, glaciers, and caverns.

Talk about being able to respond to the writing prompt, *How I spent my summer vacation.* These kids could write for an entire semester! What an experience! What an education! What an unforgettable way to learn!

Experiences: When you read about something in a book, you gain what is called *head knowledge*. But when you experience what the book is telling you, you gain *hands-on knowledge*. The latter beats the former any day of the week. When you've had an experience, it sticks with you the rest of your life.

I'll never forget the first time I went scuba diving. I had taken a course at our local aquatics center and was ready for my *check out dive*. We drove down to Florida for the weekend wreck dive. I was really excited and looking forward to it like a kid on his birthday. On the way down, we stopped at an abandoned quarry and went through all our checks. I was certified to dive at that point. The water in Florida was absolutely beautiful! We went down about thirty feet and found a sunken merchant ship. It was broken in half and lying on its side. We spent about half an hour touring the ship. It was all I could do to control my breathing and not drain my tank. On the same dive, I also saw a small shark and a stingray. I don't think any of us stopped talking all the way home. I can easily say it was a trip I will never forget.

I took flying lessons when your mother and I first got married. I had a good instructor and always looked forward to heading into the clouds. The first time you take off is such an exhilarating feeling. As the earth drops away, a feeling comes over you that says, *Wow! I'm really flying!* We did bank-turns, touch-downs, take offs, stalls, and emergency procedures. It was an awesome experience! Unfortunately, I ran out of money before I gained enough experience to get my license.

I told you about my experience at parachuting. I'll never forget it as long as I live. Somehow my buddy Mark and I decided to investigate an advertisement that I came across regarding parachuting. We went through the course that morning and in the afternoon found ourselves in the back of a Cessna ready to exit. We were up about 3,000 feet and hooked to a static line. Theoretically, the chute would open for us. All we had to do was jump. To this day, I still remember the commands that I was given. *Stand up.* All I had to do was stand and get in the open doorway. *Step out.* This is where I was to step out on a small board and grab onto the wing strut. If there was ever a question regarding whether or not you believed in God, without a doubt, this is where it is settled. *Leg up*" My outside leg was to be extended straight behind me. *Go!* Do I have to explain this one?

I let go and arched my back with my hands in front of me and spread out. I was to count to six by 1/1000ths. I'm not sure I ever counted that fast in my life. I went from 1001 to 1006 in about a thousandth of a second. I remember panicking and thinking, *It didn't work!* I crossed my legs as I had been instructed (this was to keep your chute from going between your legs), and reached for my reserve chute when all of a sudden, whoosh! My canopy came open, and I was floating to the ground. My world came back to order, and I enjoyed my trip down. I had less than a graceful landing and was more than thankful for a helmet. When my heart came back close to normal, I determined that there are some things in life that are great to do only once.

Your Mom and I have taken various classes together down at the university. We learned about gems, art, and music. We took a class in pottery and stained glass making. We learned how to do faux painting and liquid embroidery. It was a great time of learning and we had a lot of fun just being together.

Let me share with you six things that knowledge will do for you:

1. It will save you time. It will help you avoid making the same mistakes over and over. Someone has said, "The definition of insanity is doing the same thing over and over again and expecting a different result."

2. It will save you trouble. You can *piggy back* on other people's knowledge they've gained, and it will keep you from having to go through the same experiences they've had to in order for them to gain the wisdom they have. My friend Terry is missing the little finger of his right hand. He lost it while trying to clear the chute on his lawn mower that was clogged with grass. Every time I mow the lawn, I see Terry's hand, and I never make the mistake he made. I have another friend named John. John carries with him a large scar on his thigh, given to him by the mishandling of a chain saw. Whenever I use a chainsaw, I remember his scar, and I'm extra careful. The scars from these guys and others keep me from making the same mistakes they did. My borrowing from their experiences gives me wisdom and keeps me out of trouble.

3. Knowledge will enable you to talk to all sorts of people, and it will open doors for you. When you can join in a conversation on various topics it will allow you to engage in the lives of people, and it will draw them to you.

4. It will save you money. The more things you can fix around your home, the less calls you'll have to make to others to come and fix them for you. Because I built the game room and the extension on our home pretty much by myself, I saved tens of thousands of dollars while at the same time added to the value of our home. I've built toys for you kids, worked on the car, and fixed all sorts of things around here.

5. Knowledge will give you a good job. Because we understand that the more you know, the more you are valued by employers, we've put aside money for each

of you to attend college. I've read that the average high school graduate makes over $9,000/year over the drop out. The average college graduate makes over $19,000 more than the one who doesn't have a college degree. Even if you don't end up working in the field that you study for, the fact that you have a college degree will also allow you to interview for jobs outside of your educational background. It pays to have an education.

6. It will help you in the decision-making processes of life. Wise people can put together facts, experiences, and advice and have a tendency to come up with the right choices and right solutions to the problems.

Learning will never hurt you, but many people struggle in all sorts of areas in their lives simply due to a lack of knowledge."

There was no question that Tom was weaker now. He didn't want to admit it. He didn't want to give in to the truth of the disease, but he couldn't fight the fact that even though he'd had an extended nap, he felt as if he'd run a marathon. Fatigue was the only way to describe his feelings. He wanted to take another nap but knew that it could possibly interfere with his sleep later that night. *This must be what a narcoleptic feels like,* he thought. He leaned to his left and rested the side of his chin on his hand. Tom came in second to the fatigue and in a moment he was asleep again. He dozed for only ten minutes but felt better when he came to. He spun his chair around and gathered himself to go in and check on the family.

Tonight the Johnsons were coming over after dinner for a make-your-own-sundaes dessert. Later they would jump into a lively game of cards. The two couples had been friends ever since they met at a banquet for the crises pregnancy center. Tom loved being with the Johnsons. Jay and Joan were both loud and fun loving. They were constantly joking with each other and everybody else in the room. They possessed the ability to play off of each other's humor and build on the direction their mate was going in any particular area. They had two children who were close to the age of each of the Redden kids and the five of them got along easily.

The ice cream and toppings were all doled out and everyone seemed more than content to pack in the sweetened calories. Generous scoops of ice cream were doused with caramel, chocolate fudge, whipped cream, nuts, cherries, sprinkles, and cookies. This was more a night of counting blessings than it was a night of counting calories.

With desserts in hand, the kids made off to the game room while the adults found a place at the table. Laughter and gentle chiding came as plentiful as the cards and dessert. At one point, the game stopped completely when Jay explained one of his embarrassing episodes. It involved the shower at the Y, soap in his eyes, a small towel around his waist, and a miscue with an exit door. By the end of the story, the four of them were laughing so hard that both their stomachs and heads hurt. The rest of the card game went on for an hour when Tom felt the onset of fatigue once again. It was only 9:30. He was hoping to be able to stay up a little later but was learning that fighting the urge to sleep was nothing more than a prolonged losing battle. There was some small talk and love communicated between the group, but then Tom had to retire for the evening. A few minutes later, Tom was in bed, while the Johnsons stayed with Marcie about an hour longer.

Marcie felt comfortable talking with these old friends. Jay and Joan sat on the couch while Marcie took the overstuffed chair. "I know I should trust the Lord, and I do, but it's so hard watching Tom decline. I feel so helpless. I wish there was something I could actually do to help him fight this thing."

Jay sat on the edge of the couch and leaned forward. "Marcie, we're not going to pretend we know what you're going through. There's no way we could do that. But we believe your role is to be there for Tom and just love him through this whole thing. We know you're doing that, and we're committed to helping you guys any way we can."

Joan chimed in, "You need to let us know if there's anything we can do. We don't want to sit on the sidelines and not be involved. If we can take care of the kids, run errands, call people, or pray, just call us. Whatever you need, we want you to know that you can always count on us."

Marcie did all she could to hold back the tears and did a moderately good job although a few did spill out. "You guys will never know what your friendship means to me. I am so thankful for you!" They hugged each other and each re-committed to the loyalty of their friendship.

MONDAY, MAY 19

Tom did not get up. In fact, he slept until almost 9:00. They had been monitoring his sleep and found he was now sleeping over fourteen hours each day. These days, it was not uncommon for him to be asleep much more than awake. The kids were all at school and Marcie had left a note telling him she was running to the store for a few items. Tom, still in his bathrobe, stood over his coffee and read the note. It was covered in hearts and closed with the words "I've never been so in love with you as I am now."

This brought back thoughts of other notes Tom and Marcie had shared. They had both done a good job of communicating their feelings for each other on paper. He remembered a note, or parts of a note, that Marcie had written him years earlier. He got part of the note on his pillow. This led him to another part of the love letter, which brought him to the next one. When he had gathered up all the notes, he found it to be filled with love, affection, and commitment. The last of the notes contained a

$100 bill with his name on it. Also in the envelope was a hand made coupon that said, "A interlude of romance." Tom had cashed in the coupon that night.

This memory called to Tom's mind a couple of notes he had left Marcie. Both of these came from the creative side of Tom's personality and the creativity added to the emotion behind each of the notes. The first note was a secret one. In their former house, they didn't have a bathroom fan. They had to rely on an open window to let out the steam from the shower. If they forgot to open the window before they showered, the room would be filled with a fog that made it hard to see more than a few feet. No matter what they did, they could always count on the mirror being fogged up. This frustrated Marcie in particular, and Tom, on more than one occasion, had promised to bring someone in to install a fan.

Tom usually took his shower before Marcie. He was often gone before she got out of bed. On one particular morning, he showered and fogged up the mirror. When he got out of the stall, he took his finger, and with the oil from his skin, he drew a heart on the mirror and wrote the words, *I love you.* When the mirror cleared, the words were gone. When Marcie awoke, Tom was gone. After Marcie took her shower, the message came back. Tom got a call an hour later. There was no greeting. Just the question, "How did you do that?" Tom explained and Marcie applauded his efforts.

Another note that Tom left Marcie was also at their old house and was not nearly as subtle. Tom was spending his weekends putting a fresh coat of paint on the house. His Dad had taught him that every project you do outside should always be started in the back. This will do to things: it will give you practice on the side that few people will see, and, because it is really the front of the house that most people are concerned with, it will ensure that you finish the job. Tom was busy laboring on the rear of the house. Though he was far from finished with the back, he was just about through for the day.

That's when he wrote Marcie's note. With a wide brush across the far end of the house, he drew a big heart complete with an arrow. Inside the heart he drew his and Marcie's initials along with the expected *4 ever.* He finished his work of art and never mentioned it to her. On Sunday afternoon, Marcie got her love letter, and Tom received a long and passionate kiss.

His sleeping habits were not the only noticeable change they saw in Tom. The skin rash seemed to be under control but he demonstrated a sizable loss in physical strength. Under normal circumstances he could take the stairs two or three at a time. But now he never climbed more than one a time and often had to stop and gather his strength after two or three. He often didn't lift his feet high and had even stumbled slightly two or three times. Fortunately, each time he was able to catch himself before incurring any injury. Though he could still type, he noticed his speed had dropped off and sometimes he had a little trouble with his coordination. Another change seemed to be taking place on his palate. He could taste most foods as he always did, but certain foods only gave him a hint of taste. Because of this, he tended to avoid them and ate them only out of necessity and not out of desire. He and Marcie made sure they noted each of these changes in the vinyl notebook provided by the clinic. They weren't sure if these changes were a response to the treatment or the disease. Their job was just to note the changes, not make the evaluation. They did their job as best they could.

The afternoon brought them to Matt's Riley's office. They had dropped off their noted changes at the clinic and were now seated across the desk from their doctor and friend. Matt explained to them what was going on. "Your last lab results don't show any change except that the disease seems to be picking up speed. There is a civil war going on inside your body. The bad cells have launched an all-out attack on the good cells. The good cells have only been in a survival mode. They've been sustained by numbers and by reinforcements.

They have not mounted a counter-attack. Up until this time, they've been able to hold their own, but now it seems like the numbers are beginning to strongly favor the bad cells."

Both Tom and Marcie simultaneously shifted in their seats. Matt let the information sink in. After a short pause Tom asked, "How long?"

Matt folded his hands on the desk and leaned forward. "We can't say for sure. If things keep going the way they are, my best guess is about five weeks. The recommendation by the clinic is that we increase your dosage. We don't anticipate it will stop the disease but maybe it will buy you some more time. It may increase some of your side effects, but we're hoping we can deal with them as they come. We just don't know." Marcie nodded and successfully fought back the tears. She was determined to present a strong front.

In the car Tom thanked her for holding it together. He assured her that their faith would sustain them but there was something else on his mind. As she drove them home, he turned to her and said, "Marcie, not only is it important to me that you be strong, but I need your help in another area. I don't think that I'm an overly proud man. But in the process of all this, will you do your best to help me maintain my dignity?"

Tom had spent enough time visiting others in the hospital that he knew that often times they were embarrassed at their presentation in front of others. He had watched his grandfather pass away and saw how embarrassed he was over some of the exposure he had. The diapers, the baths, the feeding, and the other procedures had assaulted his sense of pride, and somehow Tom could feel how that had affected his sense of self worth. He didn't want to experience that first hand if it could be avoided.

They were stopped at a light. Marcie grabbed an overused tissue and dabbed at her eyes. "I understand and I'll do everything I can to make you as comfortable as I can both mentally and physically."

"Thanks!" he said as the light turned green and they lurched forward.

Tom managed the steps without too much time or trouble. His knees ached a little but not enough to make him complain. He was more concerned with his noticeable loss of strength and endurance. He didn't need a doctor's report to tell him who was winning the war. His entire body let him know the enemy was advancing and had the upper hand. With all this evaluation in place, Tom slumped to the couch in their bedroom. In less than three minutes he was out. He awoke three hours later to the smell of Tom's favorite— salmon. Fortunately, there were still some foods that were unaffected by Tom's loss of taste. Salmon was one of them. Marcie had just started cooking when Tom greeted her with a kiss on the back of the neck. She turned her head toward him and returned the affection.

Back at the console, Tom went to work. Could he finish saying all he wanted to say? He had no idea. He just knew two things: one, he had things he had to let his children know, and two, he had no idea how much time he had to say all those things.

#6-MAKE YOUR FAMILY YOUR PRIORITY

"There is so much confusion over the role of the family in our world today. So many people move in and out of relationships and leave nothing but rubble in their wake. They move from one venue to the next without any plans regarding how they're going to make the next one work. I don't want that to happen to you. I want you to develop relationships that are meaningful and fulfilling. I want you to have a great marriage. I want you to have a great family. I want you to have what I have enjoyed all these years. So I want to give you some things to keep in mind involving the area of your marriage and family.

A. Build Memories, Not Monuments.

The world will constantly scream for your attention. There will be times when you will have no choice but to answer that call. You will have responsibilities you must fulfill—your job, your school, the church, your friends. But whenever all things are fairly equal, and you have a choice between your family and everything else, choose your family, and you will never regret it.

About eight years ago, I was approached by our company to take another position. It meant more responsibility and much more pay. I would be able to give my family almost everything we could ever want. We would have a bigger house, a new car, all the toys and trinkets they could ever want. But in order for this to happen, I would have to make a compromise. I would have to give more of myself to the company, leaving less of myself for my family. My entire job would mean I would be traveling constantly. I would be out of our home about four nights each week.

I thought about the money. I thought about the prestige. I thought about the corporate influence. All those things were so appealing. From a professional standpoint, that's all I ever wanted. I was climbing the corporate ladder and would soon be enjoying the view. I spent a lot of time weighing the decision. I could accurately say I agonized over it. In the end, I voted for you. I knew this might be my only chance at such advancement. I knew it might be a once-in-a-lifetime decision. But I also knew I only had one shot at being with my family. I knew that whatever age you become, I only have you at that age for one year. After that year, you would be forever changed, and there would be no more second chances.

So I chose your Mom and you, and I never looked back. And each time I hear you laugh at the dinner table, and see your Mom's eyes at night, and go to your special events, or look at you as you sleep, I know two things: I made the right choice, and I could very well be the luckiest guy in the world.

That's the way you evaluate choices. That's the way you build a family. Career opportunities come and go, but you only get one shot at family. The key is to build memories, not monuments.

B. Understand Your Spouse and Children Know You're Crazy About Them.

There can be no doubt you will make mistakes as a mate and as a parent. But if your mate and your kids know beyond a shadow of doubt you are crazy about them, you can mess up in a lot of areas, and you'll still be fine.

In business, we have a book that is called a "credit/liability ledger." The credit side of the page has to do with the assets of the company and all the money that it takes in. The liability side has to do with bills and overhead. As long as a company always has enough money on the credit side to offset the liability side, the company will be healthy."

Tom's mind briefly hooked onto the memory of when he saw this happen. John was in third grade. He was caught drawing on the wall and then lying about it. When Tom got home he confronted John. John continued to deny it but reason brought the guilt home to him. In his room, Tom told him that he was angry at him for disobeying and then lying about it. Through tears, John apologized. Tom accepted his apology and then told him he would be punished by staying in his room after school for the next three days. When Tom went to leave the room, he said, "I love you John."

John just turned to Tom and said, "I know."

Back to the present, Tom wrote,

C. Understand the Season of Life You Are In.

There will be outside interests that will call for your attention. There will be lots of things you will want to do. But you must always measure whether or not you are in the right season to do them. If you want to go to school, take up golf, or start your own business, you must be able to decide if this is the right time for that. So many of the things you want to do simply have to wait until your family is in a position to allow you to do them. If you uproot your kids from their friends and family, you may very well regret it down the road. If your tee time gets in the way of 'tea-time,' you may not get another invitation. Whatever is on TV cannot possibly be as important as what goes on in the world of your family. Your kids' games must take priority over your games. There is time for recreation and fun. But for the most part, your fun must be superceded by their fun.

One of the greatest things I always appreciated about my parents was that they always seemed to be there. They were always at my events. They always cheered me on. They always had time for me."

Tom looked up at a picture he had on the wall of his study. It had hung there for over eight years, but he still revisited it from time to time. It was the picture of a little girl standing on top of a hill. She looked so much like a smaller version of Madison. The caption read, "A hundred years from now it will not matter what my bank account was, the sort of house I lived in, or the kind of car I drove. But the world may be different because I was important in the life of a child."

There was no doubt that Tom wanted to make a difference in the life of his children.

Back at the keyboard he wrote, "Families spell love, T-I-M-E. There may be a lot of things you do that you will someday regret. But you will never regret investing time and energy into your family. You are my priority. This is a special season in life. That's why I occasionally have lunch with you at school. That's why I go to your plays and sporting events. That's why I'm home almost every night. That's why we do so many things together.

Too many times people use the wrong set of criteria to measure whether or not they are doing a good job as a parent or spouse. Many times they believe they are doing a good job because they are doing a better job than their parents did. While this may be an indication, it certainly is not the correct measurement. *Better than* is not the same as being good. That will not get you to where you want to be.

The best way to evaluate your performance as a spouse or parent really is by the reflections of your children. I call it *the dorm test*. Your children are a message you will send to a world you will never meet and sooner or later, your kids will be sitting somewhere in the freshman dorm. The other students on the hall will be sitting on the edge of the beds and on the floor. The topic of home will come up and each kid will have a chance to talk about what it is like at their home. What your child says regarding you and your home at that moment will determine your success as a parent or spouse. Will they talk about love and acceptance? Will they talk about good times and experiences? Will they want to come home and bring their friends? This is the evaluation you must prepare for. This is the test you must pass.

D. Plan for Your Future With Your Spouse.

When you go to the altar, you will each make vows to the other. Most of what happens on your wedding day will be packed with emotion and celebration. Vows in that moment will be easy to say. They will be special and well meant. But after the guests go home and the honeymoon really is over, the marriage starts. Whatever your promises were to each other, they will be tested in the fires of the most concentrated form of human relationships. The ability of you to live up to your vows really comes down to two things: Your character and your commitment. Everything else hangs on these two traits.

You must understand, there will come a day when your children leave home. They will have drained you both emotionally and financially. After you have launched them into the world, what you have left of a spouse is a direct reflection of what you helped create in them. For the most part, they will have become what they are as a result of living with you. In short, if you don't like how your mate turned out, you are at least partly to blame. Don't mess it up! Hold your mate in high regard. Protect your relationship with them (even from the kids).

That's why your Mom and I try to date each week. We carve out a time for a walk, for some ice cream, for dinner, and a movie. We spend time talking and listening to each other. We developed the habit of always saying, 'I love you' before we drift off to sleep and we try to out-serve each other in love. It may cost us time, money, and energy, but it is an investment we can't afford to neglect.

Make your goal in marriage to be successful rather than to simply endure. It takes very little to get married. It takes great effort to stay married. But it takes complete commitment and an intentional will to be successfully married.

How will you know you've done it right? How will you know if you have a good marriage and family? Let me suggest two statements that both you and your spouse must affirm if you are going to label yourself a success in this area. (1) If I could do it all over, I would marry you again. (2) I want our children to have the same marriage we have.

My deepest prayer for you is that you find someone you can love with the deepest depths of your soul and someone that will love you on that same level. I pray the Lord will bless you with a sweet loving family and that you will have the skills and wisdom to pour into their lives all the love parents can have for their children. And when the Lord blesses your efforts over time, I pray the two of you will graciously grow old together and will easily recognize all the blessings God has put in your path."

Each of the children were processing Tom's decline in different ways. Madison still seemed to top the charts in difficulty. She talked to her mother and father about it sporadically as if not talking about it would change reality. She found herself opening up more readily to her friends than her family. Michelle was her closest friend. They called themselves the *M2 girls*. She was thin and had bright red hair she most often wore in a ponytail or in braids. Her broad smile revealed a mouth full of braces, and her outgoing personality brought her more than the average amount of popularity. She was the one with whom Madison spent most of her time in processing her feelings. Time and again, Madison found herself using phrases like "it doesn't seem real, it's not fair," or "he doesn't act like he's sick." Michelle always seemed to be available and even at such a young age had developed a keen ear for listening and a kind heart for understanding.

Often times, Marcie would wander by Madison's room and see the girls lying on the bed. Sometimes they would be talking and giggling. Other times they just lay there in silence understanding what the moment called for. The latter scenario seemed to present itself more frequently these days. So many times Marcie breathed a silent prayer of thanks that her daughter had such a good friend in Michelle. She understood that moving into the reality of the situation was a process and not an event, and she knew how important good friends were in that process.

John seemed to be handling things fairly well. Tom and Marcie often wondered if he understood what was going on. He seemed to draw closer to both his parents giving them a hint that he had an idea of what was happening. He was normally affectionate, but lately he seemed more physically attached. He would crawl up on his mamma's lap, give his dad a bear hug, or be more interested in just sitting around with the family.

Though they may have been unsure of John's grasp of the situation, they were certain Matty had little idea of what was going on. This was shown in the consistency of his happy-go-lucky attitude. He was still the same boy who laughed at the TV, bugged both his brother and sister, and refused to eat anything that came with the phrase, "it's good for you." He knew his dad was sick. He knew there were lots of medical visits. He understood there was more mail, more phone calls, and more friends who came by than ever before. But somehow there was an emotional disconnect between what he saw and how he understood things should be. In his young mind, daddies never went away for good. Daddies were always strong and available. Daddies were the ones who fixed things. They never needed fixing.

Both Tom and Marcie had spent time with each of the children explaining to them the possibilities that lay ahead. Along the way, they kept them updated on what the medical personnel said. They were torn between wanting to protect the children from emotional pain, and needing to inform them of the situation so as to help them through it all. It was a tough balancing act, but all in all, they did well in their measurement of information.

A couple of times each week, Dr. Matt Riley would come by to see his patient, his friend. The news was always the same. The disease was picking up speed. At this point, Tom's mobility became markedly limited. He shuffled when he walked and needed a cane to keep his balance. He spent less and less time venturing beyond the home and more and more time in bed and on the couch. Friends still came by to visit but never stayed long. They generally brought with them food, memories, comfort, commitment, and prayers. The fatigue in Tom's eyes helped them understand that he was rapidly losing the battle within, and it was their signal to close the visit. More than once, Tom fell asleep during a prayer Pastor Cobbs offered for his healing. When he awoke, he found himself lying on the couch under a blanket. As the memory of the visit came back to him, he fought with the emotion of embarrassment.

More than once, he reflected on times when he fell asleep at inappropriate times. His mind drifted to a time years ago when he went on a men's retreat with the church. The week prior had been tough and he had gotten in late that night. He emptied a plate of food, spent time in fellowship, and listened to the speaker. At the close of the evening, the men circled up their chairs for prayer. Tom really tried to pay attention. He really tried to follow along with the voices. But somehow, between the prayer for someone's uncle's wife's new job, and the need for men to step up and take a stand, he nodded off. He was certain he hadn't been out long but was equally certain that the exaggerated shake he gave himself was easily recognized by both men on each side. Neither of them said anything to him, but the smile from each of them following the "amen" gave him a hint they were on to him.

While he and Marcie were dating, they would often visit by phone during the summer. On one occasion, Marcie was explaining to Tom how excited she was to get the summer job she had. She told him about her co-workers, her hours and salary, her savings, and everything else in between. Tom was interested and wanted to know all about it. He really did. But he had been up since five a.m., and it was now close to eleven p.m. He didn't want to risk being rude, but he was exhausted. As Marcie rambled on his eyelids began to gain weight. He awoke at two in the morning to the sound of a busy signal. The phone was on his chest and a deep sense he was in big trouble was on his heart.

He remembered an incident in college, when he and Bob had joked about how easy it was to fall asleep in the library. Not a night went by when they didn't see several of the students fast asleep on their books. More than once, they left the room in laughter when a young man's mind was out but his body was in. Hilarity was always heightened when the snoring came from one of the women.

For years after, they reminisced about seeing one of their

classmates in a cubicle down for the count. His glasses were cocked to the side with one end pointing straight up. His face was pressed against a book with his mouth out over the desk. Saliva leaked from his mouth and had formed a two-inch puddle on the surface. Tom was in the reading room when Bob entered, caught his attention and gave him a *you've gotta see this* wave. Bob led the way passed the carousels and pointed down at the slumbering student.

The two of them re-entered the reading room laughing and encountering "shushes" as they came. Bob seemed to gain control of himself just long enough to pull out a sheet of paper from Tom's notebook. He took a large marker and in capital letters wrote the words, "NICE DROOL!" He held it up just long enough for Tom to read it, shake his head, and while laughing violently but silently, mouth the word, "No!" Both boys were sweating. Tom followed Bob, and they disappeared with further "shushes" from the room. He placed the paper next to the puddle made by the sleeping boy. They worked their way to the lobby and sat down on the couch burying their faces in their hands and wiping the tears from their eyes.

But that was different. All that was funny. What Tom was going through was anything but funny. He faced the very real prospect that one of these days, he was going to nod off and not come to. He understood the importance of faith. He looked forward to heaven. He knew he would soon be o.k. but deep down inside, there was a strange sense of fear that crept over him. He did his best to brush it aside, but it always returned like a loud whisper in his ear.

That night, Tom was retired for the night by eight o'clock. He slept soundly for a few of hours. Then *the dream* came to him. Up until this point this frightening vision had only appeared during his naps. Now it seemed, it wanted to be part of his nightly slumber as well. It came the same way: The meadow, the flowers, the breeze, the sunshine. They were all there just like in the other dreams. Then the rumbling started and the feeling followed. He knew it was coming. He knew he was dreaming. He knew he had to awaken. But there was no way to stop it. He ran with all his might but he never got anywhere. It came closer and closer, and he felt the fear sweep over him like an ocean wave. As it wrapped invisible hands around him, he heard Marcie's voice. "Tom, Tom, wake up. It's o.k. You're having a bad dream." Tom had been thrashing about during his moments of torment. He awoke gasping for breath and in a full sweat. "It's o.k. honey. It's o.k." She nestled next to him and put her arm across his chest.

Tom grabbed Marcie's arm and drew it even tighter. "I've never dreamed anything so real. It's incredible!"

Marcie patted his shoulder. "I'll get you a drink." She pulled from him to leave the bed when his hand grasped her wrist.

"No. I'll be alright. Just stay here for awhile." He turned his back toward her and pulled her arm around him.

TUESDAY, MAY 20

Tom was a man with a mission. He knew he wanted to complete his message to his children. He understood, without a doubt, his time was limited. It had come down to a race. He was racing to get his thoughts on paper before the end would come. He had already extended his projected lifespan by several months but could feel the sensation of living on borrowed time. His waking moments drew his mind to his computer, but his energy levels had dropped so low, it made it impossible to spend much time there. His world had shrunk to the computer, the table, the couch, and the bed.

Tom gave an audible sigh and rested his hands on the keyboard. Today's topic was almost oxymoronic.

#7-LAUGH EVERDAY

Tom was growing closer and closer to the end and laughter seemed to come harder and harder. Death is no respecter of persons and Tom never asked to be an exception. Still, he remembered his commitment to keep a good attitude during the entire ordeal. He understood, at this stage of the game what he was doing was a definite act of service and love for his children. Equipping them for success was the goal. His situation and feelings had to come second.

"In light of what's going on with me, it seems strange to write about humor. Still I know that humor is an essential part of making the ride through life worth while. There is so much humor to be found in life. Laughter is what makes it so enjoyable to be around others and in many ways is a main factor in others wanting to be around you.

When I was in college, we had a comedian come to our campus and entertain the student body. He was hilarious, and I think everybody had a great time. After the event, one of my professors shared with our class a Bible verse. It's found in Proverbs 17:22, and simply says, 'Laughter doeth the heart good like a medicine.' Then he told us about all the benefits of laughter. He said that when we laugh really hard it releases chemicals from the brain that help inhibit pain and shrink swelling. He also said, a good bent over laugh does the same amount of good to the heart and lungs as twenty minutes on a bicycle and that it helps improve the circulatory system in general. I remember leaving that class feeling so good about laughter.

The key to being able to enjoy humor is to take what you do seriously, but don't take yourself too seriously. We need to be productive people. We need to do a good job and try to make progress everyday. But at the same time, we've got to slow down a little and lift our fingers from the pressure button. Laughter is the way to do it. In the daily grind of a winner-take-all world, laughter is the pressure release valve that allows us to relax and enjoy life in general.

I'm so thankful that our family has always enjoyed laughing. I have so many memories of rolling around on the floor or putting my head down on the table and all of us breaking out in laughter. I can't count the number of times your mom and I laughed out loud just because you kids had been attacked by the *giggle monster*.

Remember the time a few years ago, when we were coming back from the beach and Matty asked if I would tell a joke? I challenged you to come up with a topic and give me one minute to tell a joke related to it. I admit that some of them were a stretch but you know I met the challenge and told jokes for three hours. Some of them I hadn't heard in twenty years. It felt so good to end a vacation with the entire car filled with the laughter of my children.

Each Christmas for several years, your mom would give me one of those tear off calendars with a cartoon on every page. Boy did I enjoy those. I even kept the good ones to send to friends so they could enjoy them too. One of my favorites was of a giant hot dog standing in front of his mailbox. He's got an open letter in his hand and the caption reads, *You may already be a wiener.* Another one that I loved was the picture of two spiders at the bottom of a kids slide. They'd made a web across the bottom and one said to the other, *If we pull this off, we'll eat like kings!* I also kept the one where a boy dog is at the front door of a girl dog's house. She's standing in the doorway in a dress. He's got flowers in his hand and he says, *Lois, I'm not sure what you rolled in, but you smell lovely!*

Tom paused for a moment. His mind flashed across all the different cartoons he'd read and somehow he remembered not only their content, but his reaction to them. Like someone entering a room, fatigue entered his body. It wrapped its arms around him, gave him a sense of warmth and in moments had him under its spell. Tom's head tilted back, and he dozed in his chair.

It had only been about twenty minutes, but Tom felt like he'd been out for hours. He shook his head, stretched his arms in front of him and glanced at the clock. His mind cleared quickly, and he set himself back to work.

"Remember going to Lake Nandina? What a great place! Each time we went we built such great family memories. I never knew a person could pack so much food in such a small basket. But your mom always made sure we had more than enough food to share with anybody who came by. We always tried to get the same picnic table by the ropes separating the deep area from the shallow end. We'd bring games and music and stay until closing. Remember the last time we were there? It was time to go home, but I wanted to make one last dive off the high dive. I built up my last dive as a great one and lined each of you kids by the edge of the water. I climbed the ladder, got to the far edge of the board and spread my arms out drawing attention from everybody around. Then I went to the back end of the board, got a good running start and hit the board with everything I had. The board recoiled and sent me skyward. At the peak of my ascent, I jackknifed and then opened up to enter the water. I hit the water with such force that the drawstring on my bathing suit broke sending my trunks to my ankles. As I sat on the bottom of the lake gathering my britches I was never more aware of how clear the water was.

During my trip to the surface, I remember wishing that something else had happened to draw everyone's attention away from the pool. Perhaps there was a car accident in the parking lot, or a couple began to argue loudly. Maybe someone's grill flared up and everyone would turn his eyes to that area. When I broke the surface, I found dozens of faces pointing in my direction and all attention focused on the guy in the pool who lost his shorts. This was evidenced by the fact that there were more than a few people pointing at me while bending over in laughter.

How about the time I suggested we do a *Chinese fire drill?* I built up the idea (your mom wasn't too enthusiastic) as we drove down the highway. I got all of your attention and explained how at the next red light we all would get out and run clockwise completely around the car. At the intersection, I put the car in park and yelled, "Go!" We scrambled out (including your mother) and made our trip around the car. Somehow though, when Matty got out he hit the lock button and we were all stranded in the middle of the road. How embarrassing! Fortunately I always keep a set of keys in a magnetic box inside the bumper. When we got back into the car, I remember your mom laughing and saying, "That was a great idea honey. Maybe tomorrow we can show the kids how to wash the car by driving it into the lake!" Of course I joined the rest of the car laughing.

How we all got a laugh out of our visit to see your mom's Uncle Ray! He had been in the hospital to have his appendix removed. The day after he got out of surgery we all went to see him. We visited by his bedside for about twenty minutes when all of a sudden he started feeling bad. No one knew what was going on until your mom looked down to see that Madison was standing on his catheter tube. At the time no one laughed, but it all came out when we got in the car. I'm glad that Madison was able to laugh about that one too. I'm sure that someday, even Uncle Ray will get a chuckle out of the whole thing.

As long as I live, I will never forget the time John was taking a shower in the downstairs bath. He must have felt as if the entire world had melted away and that he was completely alone. We could hear him singing at the top of his voice the theme song from *Oklahoma.* He was loud, lousy, and inaccurate all at the same time. When he turned the water off, he kept singing as he dried himself. I'll never forget the look on his face when he got out of the bathroom, rounded the corner in just a towel, and presented himself in all his glory to our neighbors who were sitting in the living room. I have never seen a faster case of sunburn, and we all got a lot of mileage out of that one.

Even your mom has given us episodes to laugh about. When your mom gets mad, she doesn't scream like some parents do. She talks directly and has a unique ability to confuse metaphors. She is famous for saying, 'So you can stick that in your hat and smoke it.' She also said, 'Well, I think he should take a short walk off a long pier.' My favorite is when she said, 'That's water under the dam.'

One time your mom had to go to the visitation of a member of the church. She went down to the funeral home and spent time with the family. She held herself together well, but when she got outside the funeral home, her face was wet with tears. She grabbed a tissue from her coat pocket and dried her eyes. After composing herself, she made a few stops in town. For some reason she got some strange looks from people as she ran her errands. When she got back home she found out why. A pen had exploded in her coat pocket and had covered the tissue she used. She then covered her face with the ink from the tissue and paraded around town with black marks all over her pretty face. At dinner that night, she struggled with laughter and could barely finish telling us all about her day in town."

Tom felt his mind wander again. Again, he was back in college with Bob. He thought about all the times they weakened themselves with laughter. Their personalities and sense of humor were so close, they each fed off one another and built on what the other man was saying. They would double over, sweat, and develop both a stomach, and a headache, all at the same time. It was painful but so enjoyable. Often, they would be in a crowd trying to hold themselves up as the humor took over. They turned more than a few heads as those passing by would giggle at the site of the guys. Theirs was a rich friendship built on humor and experiences and for that, Tom was ever thankful. Tom's task came back to him. He was almost finished, but had one more thing to say.

"Be careful what you do with humor. It can turn into a knife that cuts someone deeply and do more harm than good. Here are a few observations about humor.

1. The worst form of humor is sarcasm. Sarcasm has its place but it can get tiring and could cause others to label you a cynic.

2. Before you make a joke about someone, make sure that they can take it and be prepared to be the brunt of someone else's joke. If you're going to dish it out, you have to be willing to take it.

3. It is very hard to make jokes about a person's race and not be seen as a racist. Be very careful here. Don't make any joke about someone's race unless you have a good friend of that race and would tell it in their presence.

4. Never make fun of someone that has a permanent problem. This includes the disabled and the mentally challenged.

5. Know when it is appropriate to use humor and when you need to stop. The quality of humor depends on three things: material, delivery, and timing."

Tom was just typing his last thought when he heard the doorbell ring. As he pushed himself up from the desk, he heard Marcie swing the door open and shout, "Bob and Pam!" Immediately, Tom's face broke forth in a smile. What timing! Grabbing his cane and trying to control his enthusiasm, Tom shuffled his way to the door to find them in a three-way hug. In moments he had joined the group to make a four-way embrace.

The four of them had a great history together. Their friendship was built over time and laced with respect and love. They had experienced each other's weddings, birth of children, burial of parents, and celebration of accomplishments. The love Tom and Bob had for each other brought instant acceptance of their spouses. Pam was a gracious and caring woman. She excelled in keeping Bob organized and managing their home. She was the consummate supporter of her husband and encourager of their children. Tom could not have picked a better woman for such a great friend.

Marcie and Pam prepared snacks, while Tom and Bob found their places in the living room. When the ladies joined the men, conversation was animated and lively. After an hour of visiting and catching up, the Reddens filled their friends in on Tom's condition. They explained how the battle was going the wrong way, and the disease was picking up speed. They were clear in communicating how little time Tom had. Both Marcie and Pam fought a losing battle with tears, as Bob asked a question in a way that only friends could ask, "Guys, is there anything, anything, that Pam and I can do for you? Please understand how much we love you and please know this, no matter what the question is, the answer will always be yes." Tom and Marcie shared how much that meant to them and how much they appreciated their friendship and love. They related how all their needs were met and how they couldn't think of anything they needed beyond the friendship they already had.

Tom looked down as if struggling to say something. "Well, there are a couple of things that would help." All eyes and ears went Tom's way. Tom told their friends how he was writing to his children about the essentials of life. He explained his concern that he would not be able to finish it before he got too weak to go on. He told them, more and more he had to struggle against fatigue and often fell sound asleep in mid-thought. Then he made his request. "Bob, you and I go way back. Besides Marcie, you know me better than anybody. I need two things from you."

Bob leaned forward putting his elbows on his knees. "Name it," he gently said.

"Marcie and I have talked about this, and I need you to make sure that Marcie and the kids are taken care of. Do you remember that a couple of years ago, we made out our wills and asked you to be the executor of our estate?"

Bob pursed his lips together. "I remember and I'm honored you would ask me to do that. I'll make sure everything is done in proper legal order. Don't spend any more time thinking about that."

Tom continued. "I appreciate that and I just needed to remind you of it. But I also need your help in completing the project for the kids. I'm having more and more trouble staying awake and really have to fight to stay focused. Is there any way you could stop by a couple of times a week and visit with me, then type up the thoughts that I've jotted down? I know that's a lot to ask but I really need your help."

Bob reached out and put his hand on his buddy's knee. "That's not a lot to ask and you can count on me being here as often as you need me." Standing up and walking toward the door, Bob said, "I've got an idea. I'll be right back." In a moment he returned with a small Dictaphone. He handed it to Tom and said, "Why don't you just dictate what you want to say, and then I'll pick up the tape and transfer your ideas to the page?" Tom received the tool and smiled as he breathed a prayer of thankfulness for his friend.

When Tom awoke he was on the living room couch. His friends had gone, and with truncated embarrassment, he realized he had fallen asleep during their visit. He knew they would understand. Marcie told him Bob planned on coming by the next day, and how the mini-recorder was in the study.

WEDNESDAY, MAY 21

Dr. Matthew Riley arrived early the next day, bringing one of his nurses with him. Once again, she drew blood, but everyone knew this was more of a formality than anything. Tom understood most of what was being done fell in the category of research rather than treatment or cure. Matt visited with his friend and assured him he would keep him comfortable. Setting a limit on Tom's time would be nothing more than speculation.

Perry and Lorraine stopped by bringing an armful of groceries and sharing their love for both Tom and Marcie. Tom and Perry talked about all the subjects they had shared. In their years together, they had lived out a friendship others wished they had. They were friends in the truest sense of the word. Their friendship had by-passed all the barriers erected by society. They stepped over racial barriers and all the difficulties it brought with it. They never let their upbringing get in the way of their mutual love. They refused to let personality differences get in the way of them giving and receiving the love they had for each other. It was a great visit. After about an hour, Perry and Lorraine left while giving assurance of their commitment to the care of Marcie and the kids.

Tom was now sleeping over eighteen hours each day. His sleep sessions were unpredictable. One minute he would feel fine, actually good. He would feel rested and energized and ready to visit. But he never got to the point where he gave into the temptation to think he somehow was cured. The strong fingers of fatigue let him know, without question, this was not the case. For in the next minute, a wall of exhaustion would hit him with the force of a strong wind almost knocking him to the couch or bed. He learned not to fight it. He learned early on, resisting it only added to the drain on his energies. So he was confined to his home and the world of sleep whenever it would rap on the door of his body.

Without being told, the children began to spend more and more time at home and around dad. There were no more requests to spend the night at someone's house. There were no more suggestions they all go to the mall or movies. There was no more pleading to go and do all the things this family had so readily grown accustomed to. When dad was awake, they simply wanted to sit with him, share a story with him, crawl up on the bed or couch with him. Being with dad became a limited quantity and without question, each of the children knew it. These were tender moments. These were moments that love was freely given and received. These were moments that most parents and children long to have. These were moments that were too unique and too short.

FRIDAY, MAY 23

Tom was lounging on the back deck watching two hummingbirds alternately enjoy the nectar from their feeder. He always enjoyed both the deck and all that creation displayed in their back yard. He appreciated the balance in nature that he always noticed. Some aspects of nature he clearly enjoyed while others he fought against. He enjoyed the birds, the sounds of the tree frogs, the flight of hawks, and the occasional visit from a blue heron to the pond across his neighbor's field. But the battles with wasps, fire ants, moles, and cut worms were another story. He understood his role as tender of his environs but never went so far as to allow nature to run rampant. He kept his yard clean and fairly tidy and used his resources to keep the pests at bay. He struggled to keep his life in balance and made efforts to keep nature equally in balance. As he sat in a reclining chair, he smiled at the blessings he'd received from so many hours working and relaxing in their well nurtured yard—just one more thing for which he was grateful.

With his thirst calling him, Tom retreated to the kitchen for a glass of tea. From a mirror in the hall, he could see Marcie was in the bedroom seated on the edge of the bed. He grabbed his glass and sauntered into their room. He was unprepared to see his wife in tears. Marcie didn't see him enter at first and seemed quite startled when he came in. She seemed slightly embarrassed at his presence and gave a half-hearted attempt to hide her tears.

In her hands were several cards that Tom recognized in an instant. They were cards Tom had given her over the many years of their marriage. Marcie had saved them in a drawer and for some reason at this juncture in time, they had called to her.

Tom crossed the room as quickly as his condition would allow. He sat next to his sweet wife and put his arm around her. Marcie leaned toward him. His arm still carried with it a surprising amount of strength. She remembered the first time she felt that arm about her.

Tom and Marcie were on their fourth date. Although on their third date, their relationship had teetered on the brink of disaster, they had really enjoyed their time together on each of their previous encounters. Now they were heading home from a wonderful night of dining and entertainment. They arrived back at Marcie's dorm and Tom got out to walk her in. Without a word, Marcie guided him to a bench just outside the entrance. They sat for a while talking randomly when Marcie made the comment about being cold. Tom saw this as a cue and slid next to her putting his arm around her. Marcie followed his lead, leaning her shoulder and tilting her head toward him. She distinctly remembered thinking, *I think I can really get used to this.*

"I tried," she said. "I really tried. I knew these letters were in here and it's been so long since I've taken them out. But somehow I had to look at them again. There are over sixteen years of cards and letters here. And every one of them is sweeter than the one before. When I came in here I had settled in my mind that I had given you up. I had resigned that soon I would have to say good-bye. I thought I was strong. I thought I had it all together. But when I started looking at them, I realized there is no way I could ever let you go. This is not right. This is not the way it's supposed to be. Tom, I don't know if I can make it without you."

Tom wrapped his other arm around her. There was not much he could say. There was not much that needed to be said. He just held the woman who held his world together. He kissed her on the forehead and pressed his cheek against hers. He never stopped to fight the tears of his own. Together, they had gone through so much. They had laughed, cried, hoped, dreamed, succeeded, and failed together. This was yet another road they would travel together.

Thirty minutes later, Tom was on the couch. He grabbed Bob's Dictaphone, adjusted the pillows, and began speaking his thoughts for his friend to transcribe.

#8-SET YOUR STANDARDS AND NEVER WAVER

"The world is full of wishy-washy people. These people are full of compromise and never seem to reach their full potential. As you travel through life, you will need to have the proper discernment to know which voices you should listen to and which you must ignore. The voices of the world will scream, *compromise. No one will know. Everybody does it. It's no big deal.* You must develop the resolve to fight against these voices and be determined to outlast them. If you don't develop standards, then you won't have direction. If you don't have direction, then you will never know where you should go. If you don't know your destination, then you won't know where you will end up. And if you don't know what you want, you can't be disappointed in what you get.

Think about all the people of historical notoriety. When you examine their lives, you'll find that those who are held in great esteem are held there because they had standards, and they remained true to their convictions. These stuck to their ideals and refused to compromise. George Washington, Abraham Lincoln, Joan of Ark, George Patton, Martin Luther,

Elizabeth Elliot, Vince Lombardi, Harry Truman, Eric Liddell, Patrick Henry, Rosa Parks, Martin Luther King Jr., Winston Churchill, Nelson Mandela, and Billy Graham are a short list of those we hold as trophies to integrity. Nowhere in the mix do you find people who sold out to convenience and ease. We name with derision those who compromise. Names like Benedict Arnold, Judas Iscariot, Susan Smith, and Jezebel bring unified scorn in the hearts of men and women.

When I was in third grade we had a spelling test. We were sent home with a set of words to memorize and be tested on the next day. When I got to school the next day, I was prepared. At the same time, because I had always been a bad speller, I was scared I wouldn't do well.

That's when I received a small slip of paper from Tim Barnett. On the paper were ten of the twenty words that would appear on the test. I had never cheated before so this was new territory for me. Both Tim and I got caught and our mothers had to come and retrieve us from the principal's office. I was terrified! My mother lectured me and sent me to my room.

I was lying on my bed when six o'clock came. The door to my room opened, and my father entered. I couldn't even look at him. He sat on my bed, and I did everything I could to keep from crying. My head was buried in my pillow because I couldn't face the man I knew was so disappointed in me. He put his hand on my back. I remember thinking how big it felt.

He said, 'Tommy, your Mom told me what happened at school today.' I didn't answer. 'You know I'm really disappointed in you.' I just nodded my head and continued my efforts to fight the tears. 'I know cheating seemed like the easy thing to do, and maybe you even convinced yourself that it was the right thing to do. But right now, I know your heart is really hurting. I know you're probably just as disappointed in yourself as I am.'

Then he put his hand on my shoulder and gently rolled

me to my side. I can still hear the words he used. Quietly he leaned toward me and said, 'Listen to me. You need to learn something from this that will help you for the rest of your life. I know you cheated, and I know why you cheated. You wanted to do well on your spelling test. You wanted us to be proud of your grade. There's nothing wrong with that. But doing well and doing right are not always the same thing. If you get a 100% and you cheat, you will have done well, but you will not have done right.'

Then he said the words that burned deep into my heart. These are words that I have never ever forgotten. 'If a man doesn't set his standards, he can never know peace in his soul. And the peace of your soul is worth more than a 100% on some silly old spelling test.'

I can still feel his big hand on the side of my face. I felt his fingers rub the back of my neck. He told me that I would get a zero on the test and there was to be no dessert for a week. Then he leaned over, kissed me, and told me he will always love me. I remember, as he drew me close to him in a loving hug, I made a promise to myself. I promised would never cheat again at anything. And as far as I can remember, I've kept that promise.

Keeping this promise has not gone without cost. Shortly after we were married, I worked in sales for a company that sold appliances for new homes. The job was a good one, and I was doing fairly well. Late one afternoon, my manager came in with some *sales suggestions*. He told me if I made a few more promises and bent the truth a little here and there, my sales would jump at least 15%. I knew what he really wanted me to do was lie about our product. I also knew, truth is not broken by stretching it—character is. I spent a long time thinking about what I was being asked (told) to do. Compromise is never easy. I went home that night, talked with your mom, and started to look for another job the next day. You must always remember, you represent more than yourself. Everything you do, sends a message to everyone you know about who you are and what you believe. You represent your name, your faith, your family, your school, and your community.

When I was in high school, I remember reading about a man named Christy Matthewson. He was a pitcher for the New York Giants about hundred years ago. He had a double reputation. He was both an accomplished pitcher, and he was an honest man. Everyone knew he could count on Christy both as a player and as a person. During one particularly close game, Christy was on third base. The manager called for a squeeze play. When the time was right, Christy tore off for home. The entire plate area was covered with dust. The umpire couldn't begin to tell what happened.

The officials had a conference. They decided that Christy should make the call. What pressure! Christy walked around home plate dusting himself off. Finally, he removed his cap and said, 'He got me.' In the locker room, everyone wanted to know why Christy gave away the secret. Without hesitation, he turned to his teammates and the reporters and simply said, 'I'm an elder in the Presbyterian church.' Christy Matthewson understood the value of adhering to uncompromising standards. He's the kind of man I would never hesitate to trust.

Holding to a standard is not always easy, nor is it always fun, but it is always right. You must realize, truth is not something that is decided by the majority. If everyone does something, that doesn't make it right. If no one is doing a particular thing, that doesn't make it wrong."

Tom adjusted the pillows on the couch. It almost seemed like he was adjusting himself to what he was about the say. From the outside, it was easy to see there was a discomfort inside.

"When I was first told I was sick, I went through an entire gamut of emotions. Of course I didn't believe it. But as reality took hold of me, I knew I had to make some decisions. I had to develop some standards regarding how I was going to handle all of this. So early on, I made some choices and I've been determined to live by them:

1. I will carry my own burden — I will not blame anyone else for this.

2. I will not complain.

3. I will never stop loving those around me.

4. I will smile every day even when it's hard.

5. I will <u>never</u> give up.

These are self-imposed standards, and I am committed not to waver from them."

Tom turned the recorder over. He noticed the wheels were still turning. He flipped the rewind button and replayed his last sentence, "I will never give up." Satisfied that all he said was recorded, he turned the machine off and fell asleep.

Tom slept for about an hour when the dream started up again. Everything was exactly the same as it had been. The colors, the sounds, the scenery were all the same. And just as it had been before, the fear started again. And just like before, Tom was unable to get away. Like a large black cloud blocking the sun, whatever was coming moved over the top of him. And just like so many other times, Tom awoke with a shutter. He breathed heavily and wondered if he would ever get used to it. Deep inside he somehow understood this fear was a fear that was to be with him for the rest of his short life. In time, he gathered his strength and wandered into the kitchen for a snack.

Marcie came in with Madison close behind her. They greeted Tom with a hug and Marcie noticed the back of Tom's shirt was damp. "The dream again?" Tom nodded but the look on his face told her that although he seemed calm, the dream caused him every bit of mental anguish as before. "I'm sorry honey. Was it the same as before? Again Tom nodded. She grabbed his hand with both of hers. "I wish there was something I could do. I really do."

Madison sided up to her dad and wrapped both arms around his waist. "I sure do love you Daddy!" She gave him an extra squeeze. Tom took both his arms and embraced the two sweetest women in his life.

He tipped his head back to stay the tears, gave a deep sigh, and said, "I feel like I'm the luckiest guy in the world."

An hour later, Bob and Pam walked in with the rest of the Redden kids in tow. Both boys headed for the refrigerator while the couple unloaded their arms. They brought a couple of grocery bags full of food along with some fresh fruit. On top of the bag was a cluster of bananas. Bob pulled the group out and said, "We don't necessarily have to eat these ya know." Tom immediately knew what he was referring to. Both of the women had heard the banana story several times during their married lives. Still, every time the story was told it brought new details and higher levels of laughter. The four of them sat in the living room while the three Redden kids ate at the kitchen table strategically positioning themselves to catch every word of a story they too had heard before.

Both Tom and Bob filled in the details of the *banana episode*. During their senior year, the young men had assembled a *potato gun*. It was made of PVC pipe with one end open and the other sealed by a threaded cap. A mini potato was placed in the open end, ether was sprayed in the opposite end, and then quickly resealed. An electric igniter was mounted above the cap. When the ether was lit, it sent the potato sailing several hundred feet. They spent about forty-five minutes and an entire bag of small potatoes sailing small potatoes across the college lake. The two twenty-one year olds laughed like little boys who were ringing doorbells and running away.

When the potatoes were gone, they put the gun in the car and drove to the market for more *ammunition*. In the grocery store, along with a bag of mini- potatoes, they purchased some fruit to see how it would launch. They bought small oranges, tomatoes, and bananas. On the way back to the college they turned the car into an assault vehicle by targeting every road sign and several mail boxes as they passed. The tomatoes broke up while exiting the gun but still managed to leave a good size pattern on street signs. Before they got to the lake, they loaded and launched a banana. Because it was curved, the banana didn't fit well and had to be straightened out in the barrel. An umbrella was used to stuff it a good ways down the tube. They decided on a parked car up ahead and prepared for the *drive-by shooting*. Because Bob was driving, it was understood, he was in charge of giving the *fire* command.

Tom filled the canister with ether, and placed his hand on the *trigger*" with the barrel resting on the sill of the open window. They slowed down as they approached the enemy vehicle, and just when they were along side of it, Bob gave the orders to release the projectile. The gun launched the fruit and it traveled about ten feet before hitting the driver's door panel and sending *shrapnel* in every direction. It was a direct hit and through their laughter, both boys agreed the mission had been accomplished.

Not completely satisfied with the *banana pattern,* Tom decided a soft banana would leave a better mark. So he took the next banana and began rolling it between his hands to soften it up. When it was significantly gooey, he reloaded for the next assault. Up ahead they found their target—a UPS delivery truck. As they approached the brown truck, they noticed the driver leaving a home, and quickly walking back to his vehicle. It would be close, but the soldiers knew they were still in good position to complete their mission. With the window down and the edge of the barrel on the door, Tom awaited his orders to open fire. That's when things went wrong, terribly wrong.

Just as they were alongside the truck, someone in a yard behind them yelled (to someone else), "Hey!" It was just one word, and it wasn't even meant for the boys. But that word caused Tom to look back. When he did, the mounted gun moved from its perch while somehow Tom's finger hit the igniter. The gun belched out the banana and the missile hit the object it was aimed at—the interior of the windshield of Bob's car. When the banana hit, it exploded across the entire windshield and pelted the boys with chunks of banana. They had soft banana in their hair, on their faces and in their noses. Bob even found a small piece in his right ear. Subsequent attacks were abandoned, and the boys raced back to the *barracks* for showers and R & R.

It was a great story, and although everyone had heard it before, it somehow changed slightly enough to warrant the full attention of the audience. When the laughter died down enough for Bob to talk, he said, "That's nothing." You should have been there for *assassination' night.*"

Immediately, Tom knew where Bob was going and just as quickly interrupted. "I don't know if the kids need to hear about that one." But amid the mixture of protest and encouragement from his children, Tom felt compelled to let "Uncle Bob" turn the story loose.

Again, it was their senior year, and on this particular Saturday night and there was almost nothing happening on campus. A bunch of the guys were in the dorm watching what they all agreed was a *lame* movie. They decided a road trip to the omelet house was in order. Two of the boys retreated to their rooms for cash. When they met up with the other five young men, they found their plans had been changed. The five boys downstairs had decided that it was an adrenalin rush they really needed. That's when the plans for a mock assassination were made. Instead of a *drive thru* they were headed for a *drive by.*

In town, it was close to the time for the third shift to start. There was always a group of twelve to fifteen "mill workers" on the corner waiting for the bus. The boys had everything they needed: an audience, a van, a car, ski masks, and a shotgun complete with blank cartridges. Because he was the best runner (if anything went wrong) Joseph was chosen as the target. At just the right time, Joseph, complete with a trench coat and hat, came strolling by the bus stop. As he made his turn, tires were heard squealing around the corner. A sedan came by the victim and two shotgun blasts sent him to the pavement. On the heels of the assault, a van pulled up and two masked men jumped out, grabbed the man, threw him in the open door of the van and sped away amidst screams from the onlookers. "They just shot that boy! They just killed that boy right in front of us!"

The most dangerous part of the night involved driving back to campus safely bent over in convulsed laughter. The boys were sworn not to tell anyone until they had their diplomas safely in hand. Although there was some suspicion, not one of the boys gave any indication they knew anything about the *killing*. Still, those who were guilty would occasionally give a knowing smile when they caught the eye of another accomplice.

The kids howled in laughter. They couldn't believe that their dad would be in on such *cool things*. The questions they asked were followed by their pleas for more stories and "Uncle Bob" was happy to oblige.

A couple hours later, Tom awoke on the couch with Matty nestled in the crux of his arm. He looked at his young boy and thought about how small and handsome he was. It was a great feeling to have his son sleeping so soundly by his side. For a full fifteen minutes, Tom lay there enjoying the warm feeling of innocence resting on his chest. He didn't want to move, but the need for the bathroom was stronger than the peace he felt in his heart. He gently slid himself from his son and slowly walked away.

Tom was now forced to use a walker. He hated that thing. It was a symbol of age and inability. He knew he was sick. He knew he was dying. But the walker seemed to be a signal to everyone the war was being lost. He also knew that without the help of the walker, there was a good chance of falling. So he resigned himself to it and accepted it along with everything else in his life that was out of his control.

SATURDAY, MAY 24

Tom's slumber time now amounted to about twenty hours each day. He was determined to finish his project before he finished his life, so his waking hours consisted totally of visiting with guests, when he could, and recording his thoughts on the Dictaphone. Tom walked the familiar path to the couch to begin his ninth admonition.

#9-KEEP YOUR PROMISES

"There is a great tendency to judge others by their actions while judging ourselves by our intentions. But the fact is, people will judge us not by what we say, but by what we do. Your actions will always out shout your words.

I learned this lesson very early in my life. When I was about nine years old, there was a drive in our school to collect money for the county orphanage. When the cards came by, I pledged to give two dollars. I had twelve dollars, so I thought this was a generous sum. Then the carnival came to town. My heart was torn. I wanted to give what I pledged, but I also wanted to ride every ride they had. I had heard all the stories, and I knew those little boys and girls needed all the help they could get. But the carnival was coming. I thought, *Surely others would be giving. My little dollar won't matter that much.*

That's when I compromised. I knew I had to give something when the large envelope was passed around the classroom. No one knew what I had pledged, so I put in one dollar. That Friday night I met my friends in town. The carnival seemed bigger and better than I ever remembered. We rode all the rides and ate all the snacks we could. I honestly had the best time of my life.

But when I went to bed that night, the reality of my compromise went with me. I struggled to fall asleep and when I did sleep, it was a restless sleep. I knew I had not lived up to my word. I knew that I had put my pleasures and desires ahead of those kids. I knew I had to do something about it. I also knew I was broke. Every cent I had was spent on adrenalin rushes and junk food. I was a miserable young man.

I never told anyone about my compromise. I never let on that I was a little boy living with turmoil inside. For a full year I lived with the regret of my decision that would revisit me with pangs of guilt. When the drive for the orphanage came again the next year, I pledged and gave more than double what I pledged the year before. My hope was, this would lift the guilt that I had been carrying. In some ways it did. But I will never forget the struggle I had that year. It wasn't about a dollar. It was about not keeping my promise. I made another promise that year. I promised myself, if I ever gave my word on anything again, no matter what happened, I would keep it.

A couple of years ago, I had to teach you kids this same lesson. This mostly involved Madison and John. You somehow had developed the habit of promising to do things and then not following through. Sometimes it involved cleaning your room. Other times it was about doing a small chore or helping your mom after school. You would promise to do things and then let it go. It was very frustrating to your mother and me. We had to come up with a plan that would help you understand the importance of keeping your word.

So one Friday, before I came home from work, I called and talked to each of you. I told you not to make any plans because we were going out to get burgers and ice cream. After that, we were going to see the newest release at the theatre. It was going to be a great night, and each of you was duly excited. Your Mom built it up over the next couple of hours, and by the time I walked in the door you had worked yourselves into a frenzy.

I walked in, said hi, changed my clothes, and got ready to leave. I announced to all of you how I was invited to Perry's for steaks and would be home about ten. You would have thought a bomb went off in our house. All of you were livid. You complained, you cried, you even yelled. I just shrugged my shoulders and told you 'I changed my mind,' and left. At breakfast the next morning, there was a noticeable cloud over our house. None of you kids were talking to me. You were mad, and you intended to let me know it. I had lied to you. I broke my promise. You never knew it but all of this was killing me.

After breakfast, your Mom and I sat down with you and asked you how you felt about what happened the night before. Not one of you hesitated to share your feelings. Then we explained to you how we had planned the whole thing in order to drive home the point that when you break your promise, it always hurts. Slowly, the message started seeping through. The lights in your minds started coming on. You got it. To the best of my knowledge, each one of you has done a good job at keeping your word. Mission accomplished!

Keeping your word is not always easy, but it is *always* right! I've had to go back to this edict many times in my life and have had to decide that I want to be known as a man of my word. I want each of you to understand what I am about to say. Over sixteen years ago, I stood before, a room full of friends, family, and a minister. Beyond all that, I stood before God, and I promised I would love your mother and I would stay faithful to her. Know this for sure: I never once have broken my promise to her. I have never been unfaithful to your mother. You children have the power to say for the rest of your lives, your father was faithful to your mother. I'm not claiming that our marriage is perfect, or I'm a perfect husband. But I am telling you, fidelity is a hallmark of our relationship.

I remember several years ago watching Phyllis George interview Roger Staubach. He was an outstanding quarterback for the Dallas Cowboys. He is also a committed Christian. The interview was very typical until Ms. George blitzed Roger with this question: 'Roger, how do you feel when you compare yourself with Joe Namath, who is so sexually active and has a different woman on his arm every time we see him?'

Roger shifted in his chair and looked right back at Phyllis George. Without flinching, he said, 'Phyllis, I'm sure I'm as sexually active as Joe. The difference is that all of my activity is with one woman.' That's a touchdown any way you look at it. Roger Staubach is a man who can be trusted both at home and away. He's a guy who knows what his word is and knows the importance of keeping it. I would play on his team any day!

Shortly after we were married, I read a story about a newlywed couple that was on their honeymoon. Everything went well until she was struck by lightening. She lay in a coma for two weeks and then awoke. She had brain damage and would need special care for the rest of her life. That man had a choice. Two weeks prior he had committed his life to his bride. But that was before his bride had changed so much. That was when there was so much hope for their future. That was when life was good and times were happy. Now this. In our culture of selfishness, no one would blame him if he walked away.

He spent an entire night thinking about his options. What should he do? How could anyone expect him to care for an invalid wife? He wasn't planning on this. He wasn't equipped to do this. Still, he remembered his vows: *In sickness and in health.* By morning he had made up his mind. He brought his wife home with him and has been taking care of her every need for the last twenty-two years! Now that's a man of honor! That's a person you can count on! That's a hero!

I saw another hero displayed in the movie, *Last of the Mohicans*. Do you remember watching it? A tribe of Indians had attacked the British forces. A few people had escaped but were being tracked by the Indians. There was a woman named Cora and an Indian named Hawkeye, who were in love and had escaped. When the attacking Indians were about to catch them, he knew he and the other men would be immediately killed. He also knew the women would be spared and kept as prisoners. So he had to escape and rescue her later. I'll never forget the words that Hawkeye screamed to Cora just before leaping through a waterfall. 'You stay alive! I will find you no matter how far, how long it takes...' He kept his word and later in the movie, he rescued her. What a romantic story. What a giant of a man! If I was in a war, any war, he's the kind of guy that I want fighting next to me. He's the kind of guy you can count on.

In an age where the spoken word means so little, make it a point to have your word count. Make sure that your word binds you to your actions. When you do that you'll find several things happen:

1. People will trust you—you can be counted on.

2. People will have confidence in you.

3. It will keep you from having to make a decision. Your mind will already be made up.

4. It will make your behavior consistent.

5. It will give you a great reputation.

6. It will help you sleep at night.

It's real simple. If you give your word, keep your word no matter what it costs you and no matter what the consequences are. Remember, no matter where you go and what you do, at the end of the day, your heart is always with you. If you keep your word, then your heart is free to beat in peace."

Tom checked the recorder and found it to be in fine

working order. Assured of this, he felt free to succumb to the assault of fatigue. He gently placed the recorder on the floor next to the couch and drifted off. Not long after he dozed, Marcie came in and covered him with a blanket.

After sleeping for a couple of hours, Tom was once again revisited by *the dream*. Somehow the dream was a little different this time. The grass seemed greener and the flowers looked like they were bigger and more luxurious. There was something richer about the meadow itself. It looked bigger and the hills seemed to roll more gently. Tom looked at the beauty of it all and saw himself spinning slowly in a circle so as to take in the entire landscape. That's when the peril began.

There was a thumping that was coming. Whatever was moving toward him was bigger and more aggressive than before. Tom wasted no time in trying to escape. He grabbed at his legs in order to help them come off the ground. The sludge he was running in felt like it was hardening about his lower legs. He moved his arms as fast as he could, flailing like a man swatting bees. Nothing was helping.

The sound got closer and closer. He could feel it right behind him. He could sense it was just about to grab him and pull him to who knows where. He struggled with everything he had. Just when the end was about to come, he sat straight up with a start. He was breathing heavy and had beads of sweat all over his forehead. Immediately he realized it was the dream, and began to calm down.

Needing some water, he reached for his walker in order to make his way to the sink. He pulled his walker to himself but then found that he couldn't pull himself to the walker. He pulled at his legs willing them to move but somehow they were too weak. *What had happened? How could he have lost so much strength in such a short period of time? Perhaps they were just asleep. Maybe in time they would wake up, and he would be able to move.*

Tom concentrated on each leg. He found he could get some movement out of each of them, but only very little and only after great effort. He hoped with everything he had, they would come back to him, but secretly he knew it was the next phase in his struggle.

When Marcie came in she found Tom sitting upright. At first she didn't realize he was having such difficulty. She came to him, gave him a hug from behind and with one glance at his face, knew something was wrong. She made her way around the couch,

"Tom, are you o.k?"

"I don't know. My legs don't work. I can feel them, but I don't have any strength. It's like they're asleep, but I don't have that pins and needles feeling."

Marcie knelt down and rubbed his thighs. "Maybe it would help if we increased the circulation." Tom joined her in rubbing his legs. In time, he felt some strength return, but it was easy to tell that something big had happened. Something was wrong. Bad wrong.

Marcie looked at him. "I think we need to call Matt. I'll get his number."

She got up and raced to the phone.

Two hours later, Matt arrived. By this time, Tom's legs had gotten a good bit stronger. He could stand now, but walking was nearly impossible. Matt gave him a thorough examination. Nothing he saw gave him much of an answer. He scheduled Tom to come by the office later in the day. He had been planning on giving him a blood transfusion the following week, but this event moved his plans to the front burner. He knew his good friend was dying, and he was being forced to watch it happen.

Tom got his transfusion and felt decidedly stronger. His walking was coming back, but it was extremely slow and clumsy. They stopped at the medical services center and rented a wheelchair. This was a sign of them stepping down to the next level. If Tom hated the walker, he detested the wheelchair.

MONDAY, MAY 26

The next two days involved lots of visits from friends. Sometimes Tom was asleep. When that happened, the guests spent a little time with Marcie and the kids making sure they understood they were loved, and checking to see if they had everything they needed. Tom was now only awake for about two hours each day. The only pain he felt was due to the frustration he was experiencing as he watched his life ebb away. He kept his word, and he complained little, smiled everyday, never stopped loving those around him, and never gave up. His three children spent almost all their time at home waiting for a few minutes with dad. He enjoyed holding each of them and regretted the feeling that came, calling him to sleep. Often, when he awoke, the four most precious people to him would be right by his side.

WEDNESDAY, MAY 28

Tom awoke with a surprising amount of energy. He was able to stand, though not for long, and he even took a few steps. Still, his destination was the wheelchair and he pushed himself to the living room. His upper body still possessed enough strength to enable him to transfer from the chair to the couch without too much trouble. Once on the couch, he found his recorder and notes and immediately set to work.

#10-LEARN THE FINE ART OF TRUE FRIENDSHIP

"No matter where you go and no matter what you do, you will have a great tendency to evaluate your life in light of the friends you have. Both the quantity of friends as well as the quality of friends will be the determining factors in labeling your life a success. We spend so much time and energy riding the merry-go-round and reaching for the brass ring, that we fail to realize, it's the friends on the ride that make it all worthwhile.

I've gotten a good formal education, and I'm so thankful for it. But if there was any one thing lacking in my educational experience, it is in the area of people skills. I've come to find out, your ability to get along with people will enable you to be successful in all areas of your life.

There is no question in my mind, your mom is the best friend I could ever hope for. If I could go back in time and script out what I needed in a friend, your mom would outdistance anything I could come up with. We've been through hard times and we've been through great times. No matter what happened, our love stayed strong, and we remained loyal to one another. My only hope is that each of you find a mate who will be as good a friend to you as your mother has been to me.

Make no mistake about it, there are only a minimum number of neutral relationships. Your friends will either make you a better person, or they will make you a worse person. I've seen it happen in my life, and I've seen it happen in countless other lives. It just seems to be a natural law. You become what you surround yourself with.

Remember how your Mom and I tried to get this point across to you? Mom made a batch of chocolate chip cookies. She offered them to you after dinner. Each of you was ready to grab a few until Mom added something to the offer. She told you that just to play a joke on you, she put just a little bit of dog excrement, in the batter. It was only a little and she was sure that it hadn't been mixed in thoroughly. She held the plate in front of you, but for some reason couldn't get any takers. At that moment we realized you understood how just a little exposure can cause everything to be ruined. You also understood how that can happen in the relationships you build."

Tom remembered when this was illustrated in his own life. When he was in seventh grade, a new boy moved into town. Tom met him during one of his classes the second month of school. His name was Freddy Stetson. Though only a little bigger than Tom, he was a good bit more muscular. He wore new clothes, large boots, and a garrison belt with a buckle that he carried on his left hip. The rumor was that he had transferred to Tom's school because he got into a fight and put another student in the hospital. Another rumor had it that Freddy carried a knife and wasn't afraid to use it.

While no one knew these things for sure, no one felt comfortable asking him about them. But somehow, before long, Tom became friends with Freddy. Freddy was cool. He used foul language, rebelled against the teachers, and even smoked cigarettes. Although Freddy lived in the next town, they spent a good bit of time together after school and even hung out with each other on the weekends.

They climbed trees, threw rocks in the pond, and climbed in the window to explore the old abandoned Greely mansion. It was in the house that Tommy got a close up view of how violent Freddy was. He watched with a mixture of wonder and admiration as Freddy threw an old chair out an upper story window. Next, Freddy put a couch through a wall by running behind it and sliding it the length of the room, until it crashed, destroying both the wall and what was left of the couch.

On one occasion, the boys came close to getting into a lot

of trouble. They were at the mall. They wandered in and out of stores with no intent of purchasing anything. They were looking at some watches, when Tommy thought for sure he had seen Freddy slip one of them into his pocket. He didn't say anything, but was determined to keep a close eye on his *friend*.

A few minutes later, he knew he had seen Freddy pocket a lighter and a CD. The two headed for the door when a security guard stepped toward them. They bolted from the establishment and ran through the crowded mall with the guard on their heels. They split up and eventually lost him.

That night, Tommy got little sleep. He knew it was wrong. He knew what his father would say. He knew, if they got caught, he would be held just as responsible as Freddy. At school the next day Freddy laughed about it and talked about when they would return. But for Tommy, there would be no return. Slowly over time, he distanced himself from Freddy with the excuse that he had a lot of things to do. Within two months, Freddy was gone. More rumors came out that he had gotten caught robbing a home, or stealing a car. Tommy didn't know for certain if any of them were true, but he was sure all of them could be.

"It is very important for you to develop your people skills in such a way that you have enough discernment to choose good friends. The world will tell you what to look for when choosing friends. Don't follow the world's pattern regarding what to look for in a friend. The world will tell you it comes down to looks, popularity, brains, strength, money, or humor. Instead of putting so much weight on these things, look instead at the person's heart. It is there you will find a person's character, and it is in a person's character that you will find a true friend.

They will make or break you. They will bring you up or take you down. Here are some things that will happen to you when you find true friends:

1. True friends will bring out the best in you. They will influence you in such a way that while you are with them, you become a better person.

2. True friends will have time for you. They are never too busy for you. They will change their schedule for you and be there for you.

3. True friends will invest in you. Bob and I have a phrase we often use with each other. You may have heard us say it. *If I got a dollar, then you got a dollar.* With true friends, the answer is always *Yes.* As you go along in your relationship, you fill in what the question is. I saw this happen with Bob, when I was between jobs. We were struggling financially and I was really concerned. Without my telling him, Bob sent us a check. It was big enough to cover our mortgage for the next month. I still have the note that was attached to it. It said, 'Please allow me to bless you! This is not a loan. Your forever friend, Bob.'

4. True friends cheer for you. They go with you in your struggles and encourage you. They are there when you win and in your victories, they celebrate with you.

5. True friends advise you, and always have your best interest at heart. In high school, they were putting on a talent show. A whole bunch of kids were going to be in it. Not wanting to be left out, I signed up to sing a solo. I was going to sing *Unchained Melody* by the Righteous Brothers. I practiced long and hard and had all the words and timing down pat. Three days before the big performance, my friend Dave was over at our house. We were hanging around in my room when he came across my tape. He asked me about it and I told him my plans. He talked me into singing a little bit of the song with a promise that he wouldn't laugh at me. When I finished, he didn't laugh, but he did save my neck. He told me that if I sang that song, I would be booed off the stage. He was gentle about it and said it was a hard

song to sing and suggested I try something else. I almost ignored him. Then I borrowed a tape recorder and got a chance to hear myself. After listening, I think I would have booed myself off the stage. Good friends like that can save you a lot of embarrassment.

Today, you hear a lot of people talking about something called *tolerance*. This is not a new word, but a new meaning has been assigned to it. When I was growing up, tolerance meant that you could disagree with someone, but still respect his right to hold a position. Today, to be tolerant means not only allowing someone to hold a position, but also to admit that his position is equally as valid as yours, and to embrace and even celebrate his position and his right to hold it.

This new idea of tolerance is dangerous and impossible to hold in a literal sense. To hold each view as equally valid is to say two contradictory things are both correct. This is logically impossible. If I have a view stating that only my view is correct, then if you are going to be tolerant, you must embrace my view and abandon yours. This makes no sense, and a society cannot last long when they adopt this idea.

Furthermore, nobody will admit it, but this definition of tolerance is very selfish. People embrace this view in order to be liked by everyone. They are doing it because they care about what everyone thinks of them. They want to be loved by everyone.

However, true love is not seen in tolerance. It is seen in confrontation. Because I care more about you than I do about myself, when I see you doing something that will lead to destruction, I am going to confront you about your behavior. If you are traveling down the road and I know the bridge ahead is out, I am not loving you if I applaud you and encourage you to go faster. If I really love you, I will confront you and do everything I can to stop you. A true friend will not just sit idly by and let someone destroy himself and others. A true friend confronts those who need it.

True friendship crosses the lines of color, social position, economic standing, and educational achievement. If you ever find the types of friends I've had, you too will live a life that can be labeled blessed.

Boxing was very popular when I was a young boy. I loved watching the championship fights when they would come on TV. But as I watched the fights, even as a youngster, I realized that although there were just two guys in the ring, nobody fought alone. There was always a group of people around the fighter helping him to win.

When I got a little older and analyzed it a little more, I came to see that in order for a fighter to be successful, he needs at least four people around him. He needs a trainer, a sparring partner, a cut man, and a promoter. When I stepped further back I noticed that if a person is going to be successful in life, he needs these same four types of people around him.

A *trainer* is like a mentor. They are there to give you the benefit of their wisdom and experience. They give you advice so that you don't have to make the same mistakes they made.

When I was in high school, we had a neighbor named Mr. Edmonson. He was a nice man and was always friendly toward me. One day, I was riding past his house on my bike. He was out trimming his hedges, so I stopped to say hello. We talked for a while as he kept on working. When he leaned over the hedge, his pant leg rode up and I noticed a black scar on his lower leg. I had never seen it before, so I asked him about it. He told me that several years ago, he had been preparing to go fishing. He was out in the woods collecting worms. He saw a board on the ground by an old shed. He lifting up the board to gather some worms, when *Wham!* A copperhead snake bit him on the ankle. Immediately it started to burn. He quickly hobbled home and was rushed to the hospital. He was treated and was able to go home two days later. The scar was a reminder never to do that again.

Every time I get ready to gather fishing worms, I think about old Mr. Edmonson. If I see a log or board that I want to check under, I always grab a stick and use it to do my lifting from a safe distance. The lesson from a trainer is this: in life, you can listen to someone else's experience and save yourself a lot of pain and trouble, or you can ignore it, and be forced to collect your own snake bites.

A *sparring partner* is someone who will help you prepare to fight. This can also be called an accountability partner. They are not trying to hurt you. Their job is to expose you to a degree of pain that will help you to avoid mistakes that will cause you greater pain.

You know that Perry is my accountability partner. We've been meeting weekly for over fourteen years. We bounce things off each other constantly, and we don't always agree. But our love for each other is strong enough that we can agree to disagree agreeably. I remember, during one of our meetings I shared with him about a fight that your mom and I had had. He listened to the entire story and then gently but firmly told me I was wrong. He told me I needed to be a man about it and go back to my wife and apologize. He also suggested flowers. I didn't want to do that. I didn't want to admit I was wrong. I wanted to hold a grudge. I wanted to be angry. But my sparring partner wouldn't let me off the ropes. He allowed me to get down wind of myself and in a short period of time, I came to see that he was right, and the small rift between your mother and me was removed.

A *cut man* is there to help you when the world wounds you. Boxing is one of the few sports where each participant is guaranteed to get hurt. Sometimes they get hurt badly. The cut man's job is to wait in the corner and immediately work on the wounds the fighter has. He's got to do a good job so the boxer can get back in the fight. Make no mistake about it, the world will cut you. The message the world sends is this: *you're not strong enough, pretty enough, thin enough, rich enough, smart enough, funny enough, etc. Because you are lacking in these areas, you don't measure up to our standards, and you are not as valuable as we are.*

Trust me in this; You will lose a job, make a bad grade, have someone break up with you, be treated unfairly, experience injustice, and encounter disappointments. When (not if), that happens, you've got to stagger to your corner and enlist the aid of your cut man. They will be with you. They will care for you. They will pray with you. They will love you in and through all the pain.

Bob is my cut man. When we were in college, I handed in a major term paper for a business class. I had worked hard and anticipated a good grade. Two days later I got my paper back. All it said on the front was, 'See me!' I couldn't wait for class to end. After class I met the teacher at the front of the room. There was another guy in the class there also. The professor took both of our papers and told us they were much too similar to have been done independently. He accused us of cheating. Both of us told him, we hadn't copied from each other. I didn't even know the other guy. He wasn't sure which of us was lying so he had no choice but the fail us both. I was devastated. An "F" on the term paper meant a *D* or an *F* for the class.

Bob knew I was hurt and just stayed by me. He didn't say much. He was just there to listen and help me carry the load. Then he got an idea. He asked me when I finished the project. I told him I finished my final draft the night before. He asked me if I had my notes. I didn't. I had thrown them out as soon as I completed the project. He grabbed my trash basket but it was empty. Then he raced down stairs and invited me to join him in jumping into the dumpster. The garbage men had not yet arrived. If we could find my rough draft, my grade would be saved!

We dug for almost half an hour. Then he came across a stack of papers that looked like my writing. We looked through all of it and came to my rough draft. We looked like two kids who had stumbled onto a box of candy. I grabbed the papers, hugged him, and jumped out of the dumpster. Twenty minutes later the professor was convinced and my paper was resubmitted and my grade changed.

I later found out what had happened. The night before, when I left the library for dinner, the other boy had gotten my paper from my cubicle. He made a copy of it and changed some of the wording so it seemed like it came from him. The professor saw the similarities and called us on it. In the end, I got an *A* for the paper and the class, and the other boy failed, and withdrew from school the next semester. My cut man had come through!

Bob was there when both my dad and mom died. When I got laid off, he was by my side. When I was discouraged, he stayed with me and helped me to lift that heavy weight. And during this time of being sick, I look to the corner and there he is. He is always faithful. He is always loyal. He is always ready to help. That's what a real cut man is.

A *promoter* is the one who cheers the fighter on. He is constantly talking about how good the fighter is and what great skills he has. He is always lifting the fighter up and encouraging him.

Jim is my promoter. I don't get to see him that often because we live so far apart. But we keep in touch by phone and visit when we can. He always has kind things to say to me and about me. I can't tell you the number of times a man or woman has come up to me and told me some of the nice things Jim says about me. I once asked him if he could come back to life after dying, who would he like to be. He said he wanted to be himself, so he could have me as a friend. What a compliment! What a heart!

When he found out that your mom and I were getting married, he called me and said he was struggling to decide who was getting the better blessing. At our rehearsal dinner reception, I was getting roasted pretty strongly, and I have to admit I supplied plenty of ammunition. But when Jim got up, he lavished praise on both your mother and me. If I had gone into politics, there is no question whom I would choose as my lead man. Jim would be the one. He always cheered me on and told me I could do it."

Tom clicked off the recorder. He laid it on his chest and moved into a mental position of reflection. He knew he had been uniquely blessed with good friends. His mind bounced from one name and relationship to another. He thought of Marcie and her faithfulness and love. Bob, Perry, Dave, John, and Jim jumped to his mind. He reflected on teachers, coaches, neighbors and pastors. With each name came a poignant memory of how they influenced him and impacted his life. Tom felt himself slipping from consciousness. He gently placed the Dictaphone on the floor, rolled over to his left side, and with a slight smile on his face, gave way to the sinking feeling and drifted off to sleep.

While he slept, he moved in and out of dream states. Snippets of people and episodes flooded his mind. Some seemed very real while others were nothing more than his mind bouncing through the playground called fantasy. Finally it came. *The dream* started once again. Even in a state of slumber, Tom held on to his rational abilities. He wasn't surprised at it coming. He talked to himself about what was happening. This episode was just like all the others. The meadow, the grass, the flowers, the air, everything was the same. Then came the noise of the approaching doom. As he heard it coming, Tom turned to run. Again, his feet wouldn't move. At first he lifted them with his hands. But just like all the other times, they would not respond. In every other dream, it was at this point where panic and struggle set in. But for some reason, this one was different. Instead of a mad scramble to get away, Tom turned to face the menace of his dreams. He felt it coming, closer and closer. He began to retreat.

But when he saw the outcome was the same as it had always been, he just slowly spun in the direction of the danger. And come it did. Louder and louder, and closer and closer, it came until Tom felt his chest rattle. Like a stiff wind it approached him threatening to knock him over. Along with his chest, Tom felt the earth move beneath him. Just when Tom knew this invisible force was going to consume him, he awoke with a start.

SATURDAY, MAY 31

Tom found himself in his bed. He rolled over to look at the clock and found that it was eight o'clock. He was very confused. The fact that it was light out didn't give him a clue as to how long he had slept. He struggled to decide if it was morning or evening. *Surely he hadn't slept through the night. And how did he arrive at his own bed?* He tried to sit up, but found that his strength was gone. There was no movement in his legs, and he could not move his arms without great effort. He moved his head to Marcie's side of the bed. She was gone. He called to her. In a moment she was at his side. "What day is it?" he asked with caution.

She came to him and sat on the edge of the bed. She stroked his face and grasped his hand. "It's Sunday. You slept through the entire night. You had several visitors but never woke up. Matt was here and checked your vital signs and made sure you were o.k. Perry picked you up and carried you into our room. You've been asleep ever since."

Tom was silent. He stared at the ceiling and tried desperately to process it all. *How could I have slept so long?* he thought. *What did I miss?*

Marcie put her head on his chest and held him. Slowly, he put his hand on her head and stroked it. "Are you hungry?"

"I'm starving. I also need to go to the bathroom and I'm dying of thirst. But I can't move."

Marcie stroked his chest and looked into his eyes. "Mom and dad and Bob and Pam are here. The guys will help you. I'll get you some breakfast."

"Thanks" he said.

Marcie rose to leave and get the others. Somehow Tom found the strength to grab her hand and pull him to her. She returned to the edge of the bed. He looked into the eyes of his sweet wife and said, "If I fall asleep again and never wake up, I want you to know that there is no way I can tell you how much I love you. You mean everything to me."

Marcie lost the battle to her tears. She leaned down and slid her arms around him. "Tom, there never was a woman who had a better man than you. I always loved you and I always will. Tom forced his arms to embrace her and they held each other for a long time. Tom felt his own tears slide down the side of his face. He also felt Marcie's tears dampen his t-shirt.

Finally, Tom broke the silence. "Hey Marcie."

She didn't move. "Yeah Tom."

"I know that this may not be the right moment and you may not want to hear this, but I gotta tell you something."

Marcie stayed in her place. "What is it Tom?"

"Well, I think there's a really good chance that you're leaning on my bladder.

Marcie pulled herself upright. "Only you Tom Redden. Only you! I'll go and get the guys."

After Tom was made more comfortable with a bathroom stop and a new t—shirt and shorts, he was carried back to bed.

Everyone, including the kids gathered in his room. They shared stories and laughed a little as each of them took turns talking to their dad. Marcie informed him that Matt had ordered a hospice worker to come in and look to his needs. A catheter would be used, to eliminate the need to leave the bed and any medication that Tom needed would be provided.

Tom ate a full breakfast including two glasses of orange juice. He remained awake for over two hours. Other visitors arrived and the entire family enjoyed the company. Once again, Tom slipped off to sleep.

MONDAY, JUNE 2

Tom awoke with Marcie lying next to him and his children asleep around him. Matty was stretched out on the end of the bed while Madison lay on a cot and John slept on the couch at the end of the bed. He didn't know how long he had been asleep, and he really didn't care. With slurred speech, he called to his wife, and she awoke immediately.

"How long have I been out?"

"Two days."

Tom looked amazed. "Wow! That's wild. Everything seems so strange." He saw the tube running out from under the sheets and knew that Matt had been there to insert a catheter. He was quietly relieved. He tried, but got no response from his legs or arms. He was helpless. "I can't move," he whispered.

Marcie put her arm across his chest and hugged him. "We're here for you. The kids have been sleeping in here. They didn't want to miss any time with you when you woke up."

"Good. Me neither." The children came to with the words of their father. They each stretched and came and lay with him kissing and hugging him without interruption.

Tom looked sideways toward the window. The sun was just beginning to peak above the horizon. *Would this be the last sunrise he would see? Would this be the last day he would live? Would this be the last of the hugs and kisses from his family?* There was no way to tell. All he knew was, it felt so good to be so loved by his wife and kids. He understood at that moment that he was a loved man. He knew also that his love for his family would outlive his life, and that if he could have any wish at that moment, he would spend it on freezing the moment.

Tom stayed awake for almost three hours. During that time he listened to each of his children. They talked about their favorite time with dad, and how much they loved him and would miss him. Their eyes seemed to fill with tears, dried, only to be filled with more tears moments later. There were more hugs and kisses and more memories shared. Although his speech came slowly, he was able to convey to each of them his love and affection beyond a whisper of doubt.

Before Tom fell back into an unconscious state, he asked Marcie to take out an envelope from the nightstand near his side of the bed. She opened the envelope and held it up for him to read. He asked each of the children to come close. The kids knelt by his side and he instructed Marcie to place his hand on their heads, one after another. She took his hand, kissed it and held it on Madison's head as he slowly and laboriously gave his fatherly blessing.

"Madison, my firstborn. May you find a godly man that will give you security and laughter. May all the joys of God's creation be yours to experience. May you be a bold witness for the Lord and may the world be a better place because you are in it. I pray that those who see you will be reminded of Jesus Christ. In the name of the Father, the Son, and the Holy Spirit. Amen."

Madison wiped the tears from her eyes, kissed her father's cheek and moved next to Matty, letting John slide in close to his dad. Marcie flipped the page after wiping her owns eyes and held Tom's hand on John's head.

"John, my second child. May the Lord bless you with wisdom. May He make you a great leader. May you find a wife that will share your enthusiasm and be willing to follow you wherever you go. May your life with your wife have more of an impact for Christ than it does separately. I pray that those who see you will be reminded of Jesus Christ. In the name of the Father, the Son, and the Holy Spirit. Amen." John fell on his Daddy's chest. He wept on his neck and kept repeating, "I love you Daddy! I love you!"

Tom's tears fell as fast as his family's. The water flowed down the side of his face

and landed both on the pillow as well as in his ears. Marcie had to wipe his eyes and ears as well as help him blow his nose.

When John got up, Matty climbed up on the bed and lay on his father. Marcie repositioned him so Tom could hug him with his right hand on Matty's head.

"Matty, last but by no means least of my children. May you grow strong and healthy. May you learn all the great lessons life has to offer. May your life be filled with friends, but may you find a friend that sticks closer than a brother. May your wife be a great encouragement to you and help you achieve all the goals you set. May her heart always stay with you and may you love her with an undying love. I pray that those who see you will be reminded of Jesus Christ. In the name of the Father, the Son, and the Holy Spirit. Amen."

Through his tears, all Matty could come out with was, "Oh, Daddy. Oh my Daddy."

Every family member now climbed on the bed. Each of

them wanted a piece of this man that they had come to love so dearly and so well. They hugged him, kissed him and told him over and over again how much they loved him. Tom's ears refilled with tears. Marcie had to turn his wet pillow over and reposition his head.

When the emotions had calmed a bit, Tom asked the children to leave the room for a moment. He wanted to have some time with the love of his life. Reluctantly they obeyed with the assurance that their mom would call them back in the moment they were through. With the door closed behind them, Marcie drew herself close to her husband. Tom asked her to pull another envelope from the drawer on his side of the bed. She opened the envelope and lay next to him holding the sheet of paper up for him to read.

"To the love of my life,

There are no words to tell you how much I love you. You have made my life complete, and it is because of you that my heart carries a smile. You have been everything I could ever ask for in a companion and more. I know two things with absolute certainty. If I could go back in time, I would marry you all over again. Also, if I could pick a marriage for our children to emulate, it would be ours. You have blessed my life more than a hundred fold, and I am eternally grateful to you. As I move from hear to eternity, please understand that as I said before, I will wait for you inside the eastern gate. I look forward to that great day when you and I will be together again. I love you today, I will love you tomorrow, I will love you forever!

With all the love I have, Tom."

Marcie said nothing. She placed her head on his chest and let those loving words settle in and find a resting place in the deepest recesses of her heart. Tom longed to hold her. He willed his arms to wrap around her but to no avail. He would have to settle for the mental image of embracing her and holding her close. Marcie looked up and wiped the tears from

Tom's face and followed by attempting to dry her own.

In a moment, Marcie pressed herself away from Tom. She reached over and opened the drawer of her own nightstand. Seconds later she held an envelope in her hands. Tom raised his eyebrows. She smiled at him and said, "Mr. Redden, you're not the only one who plans ahead you know." Tom gave a half smile as Marcie sat on the bed facing him and began to read.

"My Sweet Husband,

The last sixteen years of my life have been a gift from God. I realize you are not perfect, but I believe I can make a strong case against anyone who claims you are not the best. When I was a little girl, I daydreamed about marrying a man like you. You are everything I ever wanted in a man, and I believe the day we were wed all of heaven was smiling. There are people who have loved others longer and there are people who have loved others better, but I am convinced that no one can love another deeper than I have loved you." Marcie had to stop to gain her composure. Through blurred vision and a failing voice, she started again.

"The Bible tells us that to the Lord, one day is as a thousand years and a thousand years as one day. Please understand, because that is true, it will only be tomorrow before I see you again. You are my forever love and my heart goes with you into eternity.

Your forever bride,

Marcie."

She kissed him on the lips and rested her head on his chest once again. She lay there for a few moments caressing his face and neck and kissing his hands and face.

Tom felt a wave of fatigue come over him and knew that the battle for consciousness had begun. He brushed Marcie's face with his, gently kissed her turned up lips and slurred, "Better get the kids."

The children were seated in the hall outside of their parent's room. Marcie opened the door and all three sprang to their feet and entered the room without an invitation. They each climbed on the bed and kissed and hugged their father. Somehow, all five of them sensed this was the end. They had prepared themselves as best they could, in their own way, for this moment. They had said their good byes. They had expressed their love. They had held on as long as possible. And now they knew the time of letting go had come.

All four clung to Tom and joined his tears with theirs. Tom smiled one last time for them. It was the biggest smile they had seen from him in several days. Once again, the disease won out, and Tom turned his head to the side and fell fast asleep. Though there was no way to be sure, They all knew in their hearts that this husband and father would not wake up in his room but rather in the presence of God.

One by one, the family left the room. It had been a long and emotional three hours. They needed food, they needed showers, they needed time to gather their thoughts and emotions.

Over the next several hours, the house began to fill with family and friends. Marcie's parents were the first to arrive. They were followed by Perry and Laura, Bob and Pam, Pastor Cobbs and his wife Karen, and a host of others. Lastly, Dr. Matthew Riley entered. He checked on Tom's vitals and found them to be failing. His blood pressure was dropping, his breathing was shallow, and his heart rate was slowing. His medical training told him it wouldn't be long before he lost another dear friend.

The refrigerator was filled to capacity as was the pantry and the counter. Friends milled about the living room talking and doing their best to comfort and encourage Marcie and the kids.

Tom's body did not move, but his mind bounced from one

dream to another. While he was conscious, he wondered how often *the dream* would revisit him. His answer came just two hours after he began slumbering.

Just as in all the other dreams, Tom found himself in the middle of a beautiful grassy field set on the crown of a lush knoll. The air was fresh, the breeze was invigorating, and the sun was bright. Tom saw himself standing in the meadow looking around at the beautiful scenery when the pounding began. He knew what it was and he knew his reaction would be to retreat in fear. But this time, his emotions were vastly different. The wave of fear didn't wash over him. The panic didn't set in. The noise got closer and closer and grew louder and louder. He turned and faced the direction of the sound and felt no compulsion to run. It didn't matter if his feet were stuck or not. He was not going to try to escape. In a strange way, it was almost as if he were welcoming it. He felt confident and at ease. He felt at peace. He felt he was not alone. He glanced behind him and saw some type of being. He knew he had never seen it before yet it felt so familiar to him.

Although he was somewhat transparent, Tom could tell that he was tall and strong and seemed to be built like a warrior. His brown hair was parted in the middle, and was semi-wavy and drawn behind him resting on his back just below his neck. About his waist he carried a small sword with a handle that glistened with various kinds of precious stones.

Tom couldn't take his eyes off of him. As he continued to stare at this man, the man came more and more into focus, eventually losing his transparency all together. He wore a dazzling white robe made entirely of one piece. It covered his body down to his knees and was gathered at the waist by the belt that held his scabbard. When Tom looked at his face, the man looked down at him, gave a gentle smile and a slight nod of his head. He said nothing, but Tom knew, with this escort, he was safe.

The noise grew louder still, but Tom was too captivated by this strangely familiar man to pay any attention to it. Then it happened. As the noise and whatever was causing it threatened to knock them off their feet, the man reach over and covered Tom with the cloth that draped from his outstretched arm. The noise passed over them and died out completely.

When the arm was withdrawn, Tom saw that he was no longer on the hillside. Now he was in a completely different place. A feeling of peace that he had never felt before was deep in his soul. His companion was with him. He looked around and saw a large open gate. It was breathtaking in its elegance. It was easily ten feet tall, ornately carved, and appeared to be made of a single pearl. He knew this was heaven, and he knew he was finally home. It took every ounce of resistance to keep him from running through the entrance. His eyes filled with tears. But these were not the tears of sadness or regret that he had grown accustomed to over the last couple of months. There was no doubt, these were tears of indescribable joy.

Back in the room, Matt and the family watched Tom. They saw him take a deep breath, move his head to the opposite side, and exhale slowly. They couldn't be absolutely sure, but each of them seemed to notice a slight smile splash across his face. It was there for just an instant and it dissolved as quickly as it came. Matt held the stethoscope to Tom's chest. He moved it a couple of times, then turned to Marcie and quietly said through the tears that only a dear friend could shed, "He's gone."

New tears came from all those in the room. They knew where this man was, they knew the struggle was over, and they knew that at last, the prayers they had prayed for his healing had been answered. Tom now was healed from the disease that robbed him of his health.

In the living room, Marcie and the children were each embraced by all those present. Without words they all agreed that they loved this family and they would support them and provide for them both during and after this difficult time.

THURSDAY, JUNE 5

It was a warm day in early June and the medium sized church that the Reddens had become such a part of was packed. Family, friends, and what looked like an entire community, gathered to pay tribute to Tom and support his family. The service was done just as Tom had sketched. Tears flowed openly and without apology, with the tissues running out long before the tears did. His preacher, and several of his friends, got up and spoke about Tom's commitment to his Lord, his family, his church, and his friends. Words like loyalty, trust, and love were used in abundance. Memories of Tom's childhood, college days, married life, and professional life were recounted. The memories that brought tears were interwoven with stories that brought laughter. Songs in celebration of Tom's home going were sung both by soloists and the congregation.

Before the closing prayer, Perry and Bob returned to the podium and asked each of the children to join them. They then presented to the kids their own individual copy of the project Tom had labored over for the last few months. The project had been set into book form and bound. The children received the books knowing they contained the words penned by a man who loved them more than life itself.

Marcie was washed out. The long ordeal was over. As she walked up the aisle accompanied by her children and parents, she knew that her life would be different from now on. Although she was struggling with conflicting feelings, she knew deep down inside that she would heal and she would be able to move on.

At the graveside, a verse of Scripture was read, a few words were spoken by Pastor Cobb, and a closing prayer was given. While he prayed, Marcie felt compelled to open her eyes. She didn't want to. She wanted to follow along with the prayer that was given. But somehow the ability to resist was too strong. She looked up at the casket that carried the shell of her husband. And for just an instant, a mere instant, she saw something.

There, behind the wooden box was a man dressed in a flowing white robe. She saw him but at the same time, she saw through him. He was tall and muscular and she could see the handle of a sword that was slung over his shoulder. He had both his hands stretched out above the casket. He looked directly at her, gave a reassuring nod, and faded away. In that moment, she had an unexplainable peace wash over her like she had never felt before. She knew beyond all doubt that her husband was safe, and she and her family would be o.k. And for the rest of her life, she walked with that peaceful assurance.

Tom was a blessed man as well as a blessing. At the end of his earthly life, he left behind a wife, three children, and a town full of friends. Beyond that, he left a book of wisdom, a life full of memories, and a legacy never to be forgotten. Everyone who knew him understood that their life was that much richer for having spent time with Tom Redden.

POST LOG

Fifteen years later, The Redden children were grown and each had married a wonderful partner. Pastor Cobbs had officiated over each of the ceremonies and both Bob and Perry participated as well. In fact, in Madison's wedding, Perry stood in for Tom and gave the bride away.

Madison had married a man that reminded Marcie of Tom. She lived in a small town not far from her birthplace and had two girls named Whitney and Anne.

John worked as an engineer. In time, he opened his own firm and became quite a success growing the company from two employees to ten. He and his wife had a son named Tom. They settled an hour from Marcie, making it easier for quick trips back home.

Matty went on to become a high school English teacher and track coach. In just his third year of teaching, he was named teacher of the year for the county. He had married his high school sweetheart and established their home in a town adjacent to Marcie's. They were expecting their first child in three months.

In time, Marcie began to heal. The hollowness in her soul slowly filled in, and she gained the strength to accept the reality of life and to move on. She never had the urge to remarry though there were some men she agreed to spend measured amounts of time with. She still spent her time with the ladies group she had come to know and love. She filled her days with serving in the community and doing her part to spoil her three (soon to be four) grandchildren. The peace that she experienced at Tom's graveside never left and continued to sustain her all the days of her life.

ABOUT THE AUTHOR:

Dr. Jirgal is a 1980 graduate of Gettysburg College where he became a four-time conference champion, All-American, and inductee to the Middle Atlantic Conference *All Century Team* in the pole vault. He holds an undergraduate degree in health education and physical education. Following graduation, he taught on the high school and college level while coaching football and track in both venues. He holds masters degrees in health education, sports medicine, and divinity, as well as a doctorate in ministry.

He has been the director of Sports Medicine at Wingate University, area director for the Fellowship of Christian Athletes and has served on the staff of Hickory Grove Baptist Church in Charlotte, N. C., as well as leading Lakeview Baptist Church, in Monroe, N. C. as the Senior Pastor. He has served on the local board of directors for the Fellowship of Christian Athletes, New Orleans Baptist Seminary and the ministerial board of Wingate University. He currently serves on the board of directors for The Carolina Study Center, and Fathers in Touch ministry.

Dr. Jirgal is the founder and director of *The Jirgal Leadership Institute* where he strives to equip people for success in leadership roles. He and his wife Pam have three children, Joshua, Caleb, and Sarah. They reside in Monroe, N. C.

OTHER BOOKS
BY DR. STEVE JIRGAL

The Path of a
Champion

The Dirty Dozen

Dying to Live

Life Points

Principles of
Wholeness

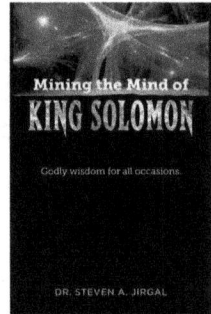

Mining the Mind
of King Solomon

Questions regarding any of these titles can be
directed to Jirgalleadership@gmail.com